Where's Opie?

Where's Opie?

Vanished in Chicago

Donald Ross

iUniverse, Inc.
Bloomington

Where's Opie?
Vanished in Chicago

iUniverse books may be ordered through booksellers or by contacting:

iUniverse
1663 Liberty Drive
Bloomington, IN 47403
www.iuniverse.com
1-800-Authors (1-800-288-4677)

ISBN: 978-1-4620-8303-9 (sc)
ISBN: 978-1-4620-8304-6 (ebk)

Printed in the United States of America

iUniverse rev. date: 12/21/2011

Contents

The Past 1

    Chapter 1   2006.................................3
    Chapter 2   2007.................................21
    Chapter 3   2008.................................37
    Chapter 4   2009.................................51
    Chapter 5   2010.................................59
    Chapter 6   2011 Jan thru Jun 83

The Present 119

    Chapter 7   2011 July thru Nov21st
                          (the 5th anniversary of
                          Jesse's disappearance 121

The Future 171

    Chapter 8 2011-   Epilogue 173
    Appendix A   The People 177
    Appendix B   Internet 191
    Appendix C   Poetry and verse........199
    About the Author 219

Dedicated to Jesse Ross and all the missing and
unidentified
And those who wait and hope for their return.

Acknowledgments

I'd like to thank Michael Tabman for his input and suggestions on writing and publishing.

Also, thanks to Jannel Rap for her help also, taking pity on an ordinary guy trying to tell a story.

A special thanks to my wife who patiently read and edited my early work, no doubt saving Me from potential embarrassment and possibly a lawsuit or two.

And lastly thanks to thousands of ordinary folks who inspired me and who are such an integral part of this story.

IN THE BEGINNING

Jesse Warren Ross

Jesse was born on February 18th, 1987 at the KU Medical Center around 4:00 am. True to his nature, he popped out on his due date!

Jesse attended 3 and 4 year old preschool at Raytown South High School, part of the Early Childhood program. We called it 'Jesse and his girls' These were high school girls who earned credits working with the preschoolers in the program.

He then went to St. Regis Grade School—kindergarten through 8th grade—and attended St. Regis Catholic Church with his family. Jesse was involved in various service projects, for example, assisting at St. Monica's daycare in downtown Kansas City. He played Soccer, ran Track, joined Cub Scouts and later Boy Scouts. Jesse loves all kinds of sports (especially the Kansas City Chiefs and KU) & would also watch Charlie Brown & Snoopy holiday movies with his Mom. One Halloween, he even dressed up as Snoopy!

Jesse worked a concession stand at a ball field in Kansas City and was recognized for his salesmanship and ability to organize. He went to Jeff City with his father and a group from St. Regis Catholic Church to support Pro-life legislation. Jesse's outgoing personality both endeared and frustrated his teachers at times. For his 8th grade trip, Jesse went to Chicago with his father and fellow students.

Jesse attended Archbishop O'Hara High School and graduated in 2005. He ran Track, Cross Country, was on the Yearbook staff, participated in the Knowledge Bowl, and was a 'Bleacher Bum' (pep club). Jesse worked for the East Glen 16 Theatres in Lee's Summit. He worked with his brother, Andy and they formed many lasting friendships with their co-workers from the theater. Andy and Jesse loved to hang out at the *Steak and Shake* with their co-workers and to preview new movies at the theatre. One of his co-workers was part of a band called *A Dead Giveaway*. Jesse became involved with the band and their family members. He traveled with the band and helped organize events. The band has become part of our extended family. Later he worked at the Super Target store in Lee's Summit. For his senior project, Jesse organized a battle of the bands and raised over $600 for the Catholic Worker House. Upon graduation, Jesse received an academic scholarship based on his ACT score.

Jesse attends UMKC, majoring in Communications, with a minor in Politics. In 2005, he went to Chicago for the Mock UN Convention. Jesse was a member of the Spirit Committee, helping to organize various activities on campus. Jesse worked for Crowd Systems, where he was able to attend concerts and sports events working as security. He was especially excited when he worked Chief's football and KU basketball games. Jesse became an intern at 95.7 the Vibe, a popular KC radio station. They created an on-air personality for Jesse, as part of the morning show *Shorty and the Boyz*. Jesse loves his music (loud) and working remote broadcasts; A job made in heaven for a 20 year old! They called him 'Opie Cunningham'. Jesse was looking forward to his promotion as a paid member of *Shorty and the Boyz* in January 2007. Also, in the fall of 2006 he started working for *Nuvio*, a voice over internet provider. Jesse was pledging the *Lambda Chi Alpha* fraternity.

This is the rest of the story . . . .

PART ONE

THE PAST

CHAPTER 1
2006

This is our letter to family for Christmas 2005. This is a picture of a family standing on the brink of disaster with no clue what is coming.

Christmas Greetings:

News flash: Don and Donna have moved to 15706 Lawrence in Belton MO 64012.

We're still unpacking but the place looks pretty much like home. The old house is still on the market so we are looking for a buyer. This has been quite a year.

Jesse is 18 and in his first year at UMKC; He works part-time doing crowd control at various sporting events (Chiefs games, KU games), concerts, etc. His car was broken into and someone got all his stereo equipment. He went to Chicago and got mugged. But the good seems to outweigh the bad; He really enjoys his work and his classes. We will be finishing our new basement and he will have a nice room down there. Jesse seems to enjoy people and has made several interesting friends throughout the community. We are constantly amazed at the things he has accomplished.

Andy is 21 and attending Longview Community college; He works for Walgreen's and has a really nice apartment in Lee's Summit. He is still interested in his music and has 2 nice roommates. He is very laid back and seems to take everything in stride.

Donna is still working at Burke Elementary. She likes having her summers off. She is excited about decorating the new house. She and Jesse love to watch the Chiefs and KU basketball.

Don is in his 30th year at AT&T/SBC. Six people got special offers to leave the company but he was no. 7 so he is still working. He has been a volunteer at Donna's school teaching English to Hispanic students. He also has accumulated 30+ hours at Longview Community College.

Earlier in the year we had a break-in and lost most of our electronics (Thank goodness for insurance). Again the good outweighs the bad. Don has a new great niece and nephew. We have a new house; we can still afford gasoline! Our boys are not in Iraq. We are all looking forward to Christmas in our new home. We hope 2006 will bring the opportunity to travel and see friends and family.

Wish you all merry Christmas and the best for 2006!

November 18th, 2006 I awoke and heard Jesse moving around the house in the early morning darkness. The clock said around 5:00 am. I remembered I had to get him to the UMKC campus by six to leave for Chicago. For the second year in a row, he was taking part in the Model UN convention and would be leaving around 6:00 a.m.

I managed to get moving; had a quick breakfast. Donna was sleeping in, as I had told her there was no reason we should both be up so early. Thinking back I now realize she would have given a lot to be with Jesse and I on that early morning trip.

Jesse in 2006, was a tall, gangly redhead, freckle-faced and quick to smile or laugh. He was a student at University of Missouri, Kansas City, majoring in communications, and minoring in politics. He was an Intern at a local radio station, and also worked for a voice over Internet Company. He was an enthusiastic joiner of just about anything.

Jesse and I climbed into the Trailblazer and made the twenty minute or so drive to the school. We talked a little; mostly he fiddled with the radio, scanning around for some song or another. He would tell me "Dad, I think you'll like this one". Usually it sounded like most of the others; an out of control noise fest, but I usually just nodded and let it go.

I exited at 63rd street, as I would have if going to work, then realized my mistake. Jesse said "That's okay, just keep going and you can get back on 71, it's the next exit."

With Jesse giving directions, I pulled into a small parking lot on campus; A pickup set in the middle of this small lot and a young man stood next to it.

I let Jesse out and then I pulled to the end of the lot. There was only the one entrance/exit, and so I turned around. As I did the pickup pulled out, And I pulled up next to the young man and Jesse. I didn't know at the time but I believe this was Ralph, Jesse's close friend. They were students at UMKC and had also attended High School together. At the moment they were engaged in animated conversation, apparently excited about the days to come. In 2005 Jesse and classmates had come to Chicago for the same event. They chose to ride the train. I delivered Jesse at Union Station and we stood around and talked for some time. He seemed happy to spend the time with me rather than looking for his classmates. However in 2006 my boy was a man; as he and Ralph seemed to talk at the same time, I slowed; He looked up, still talking to Ralph, and waved, while still talking to Ralph. I returned his wave, and not wanting to break up the conversation, I pulled on out of the lot and headed home. I think we both had the same thought; Only 4 days and we'd be back together again.

Later in the day, while driving through traffic, on my way home, my cell rang. It was Jesse. He was in Joliet Illinois, about an hour from Chicago. He was my boy again, talking excitedly about himself and the other students. He wanted to know if I knew Joliet. I said yes, that I remembered it from the *Blues Brother's* movie. We talked a little longer then I told him traffic was heavy and I would have to talk to him later. Again I had that thought, that I would be seeing him in 4 days.

Jesse called and spoke with Donna on November 20th.

November 21st, 2006 Tuesday, afternoon, I was sleeping; I had worked nightshift 11:10 P.M. until 7:10 A.M.

I was awakened by a call that afternoon., I am still hazy on the time. I hadn't really thought about it but we were supposed to get a call from Jesse letting us know he was on his way home. The voice on the phone was a stranger; He informed me he was a sponsor for Jesse's group from UMKC at the convention in Chicago. He was calling to inform me that they were preparing to leave, but unable to find Jesse. As I remember, he said he would call back when he knew more.

His name was D and he was one of two sponsors that had accompanied Jesse's group to Chicago. He gave me a brief explanation of events leading up to the time to leave. He informed me that J would be coming home soon with Jesse's things and the remainder of the group. D would remain and work with the police in trying to locate Jesse. All this time my mind was reeling, trying to take in the horrible reality. I was hoping that I was still actually sleeping and that this was just some horrible nightmare.

After hanging up, I sat, too stunned to think. I called my wife Donna at work about 3:30. I tried to speak in a calm voice, telling her to come home; that I had received a call and that they were unable to locate Jesse. She told me she would be home as soon as she could. I now feel that perhaps like me, she wasn't prepared to deal with the real possibility that Jesse had disappeared.

Waiting for Donna, I wandered out to the driveway, my mind filled with dread and praying to God that this was not really happening. Jesse's car was in the drive; I wandered over to it and saw it was as usual, a mess. I got some trash bags and began to clean the debris from the car; inside and then the trunk. I started towards the garage and suddenly I stopped, paralyzed by the horrible situation I was facing. I wanted to scream, but instead I said a frantic prayer to God: "Please don't let this be real". Some time later my neighbor told me she had been looking out the window. She had seen me in the driveway, and thought something was wrong.

From this point forward it is like an episode from the Twilight Zone. Donna came home. I must have answered her questions, but I can't remember. I called work told them the situation; I could barely hold back the tears. I also began to call family and friends. I called our Deacon Ken Albers; as I began to speak I broke down, on the verge of tears. But he began to talk to me, asking what had been done, assuring me that he and his wife would arrive soon. His cool and confident manner helped me to hold it together.

At some point in time Donna's sister Debbie arrived. She sat and talked with us. November 22nd, J arrived from Chicago with Jesse's things. He had maps and documents to show us the locations where Jesse was staying; where the meeting hotel was located—where he actually disappeared. Finally we had some information.

According to J, Jesse had left the Sheraton Inn Four Points, and walked to the Sheraton Inn Office and Towers on Water Street. He attended a party and later went to the mock UN emergency council meeting. Around 2:00 A.M. a break was called. According to Ralph Parker, Jesse's friend and roommate, Jesse got up from his chair and proceeded out the rear doors of the meeting room. This is the last time he has been seen.

The following information comes from the official police report:

Ross, Jesse, Wearing a blue hoodie with "UMKC" blue t-shirt "believe" (This description was not correct; apparently D was only able to guess at what Jesse had been wearing.) The form submitted had *AREA 3 SPECIAL VICTIMS UNIT* in large letters. The time that the report was filed showed 6:00. That would have been 6 P.M. Jesse had last been seen, at 02:30 A.M, so nearly 16 hours later the police were notified? Even if they had started looking at 6:00 A.M., That would have shaved hours off the delay. The police then began a search around the area of the hotel, by the lake, and along the river near the motel. They talked with hotel security. Hotel security people said they had seen no one of that description,(the wrong description), but added that there were 50-100 persons in the area at that time. The report states "Beat 1855 searched area near Sheraton hotel for any video surveillance cameras with negative results." We are not sure if this means they saw no camera's or they actually watched videos. We know that the hotel did have some security cameras.

A picture of Jesse in a lobby surrounded by elevators circulated and was mistakenly identified as the exit to the Office and Towers building. This was however not the case, this picture was taken from video footage at the Four Points before Jesse left to go to the meeting. After the meeting there was neither known video nor any pictures taken as far as we know. He walked straight out of that meeting into oblivion.

Let me take a moment to cover something we have had to deal with since Jesse's disappearance. Jesse left the meeting at around 2:30 A.M. His roommate Ralph returned around 6:00 A.M. Ralph saw Jesse's darkened room and assumed Jesse was there. Later in the day Ralph awoke and realized Jesse hadn't been in at all. At some point Ralph informed the sponsors. Everyone assumed Jesse had crashed in somebody else's room and the end result is that 12 hours more or less passed before anyone thought to take action and find Jesse. When the official hunt for Jesse began, The officials were involved in getting over 1000 students loaded up and home. The hotel was moving people out of rooms and cleaning up. Jesse was almost an after thought in the circus like atmosphere that ensued. We can not say who is guilty of what, if anything, but it will haunt us that Jesse could have been gone so long without someone beginning to look. And then after all this the police arrived, with no witnesses, no crime scene, no nothing.

Donna and I during this time were trying to contact our older son Andy; Andy had moved out and we often had to call Jesse to get hold of Andy. Now we had to call and email. We finally heard back from Andy, we asked if he had talked to Jesse, and he said no. We told him the news and told him to come home as soon as he could.

Personal note: Our son Andy works for Walgreens. When his boss heard about Jesse he presented Andy with a check for the reward fund. My union, Communications Workers of America, launched a national campaign to raise awareness and funds. The school where my wife worked presented us with a check. My employer AT&T made few Inquires as to what was happening, showed no interest in the reward fund; And they charged the days I was off against my vacation time; So much for the joys of working for a large multinational corporation. In fairness to my boss and my co-workers I should point out that they did join with the union in a sale and fundraiser for Jesse's benefit. Not to get too preachy, but people make the world not corporations.

The shock of Jesse's disappearance was a constant companion. I think we slept because we were drained. We cried a lot, but tears do not change anything. That may sound cynical but it is true.

Meanwhile, on November 22nd, J gave us the number for the Chicago Police. We called and made first contact with the police. I talked briefly with a detective, who asked a few questions and hung up. Later I received a call from an undercover detective who asked for details about Jesse's appearance. He was out on the street and assisting with Jesse's case.

In Belton, we had been keeping quiet about Jesse's case with the media, as we had made contact with Detective Sergeant R of the Special Victims Unit, who was apparently the lead on our case. He advised us to hold off on talking to the media until the police could work some leads. We were still pretty much in shock at this time so we were willing to let someone else call the shots.

You the reader have not seen a date or a time mentioned for recently. This gives you an idea how we felt. Time lost all meaning. We were to learn later from a wonderful counselor for the missing, about the physical and emotional drain of having a missing loved one. Our son Andy would stay up all night, searching the internet for info about Jesse, keeping a vigil.

My brother and his wife came to be with us from Wichita. They accompanied us to our local flea market to do our favorite thing, shop and browse. I remember wandering around trying to be up; trying not to cry in a public place. The company of family and friends became bittersweet; happy to have them near yet the memories they evoked were so hard to bear. My cell and Donna's both began to ring. It was the media, wanting to interview us as soon as possible. My brother and his wife felt they would be in the way, so they said good-bye. Personally I would have liked to have had them there for support, but Donna and I were so overwhelmed by the idea of facing the media, we were unable to say yea or nay. We returned to the house and there were 5 news vans parked along the street in front of our house.

Our goal in life has always been to live very quiet lives; raise our sons to live happy lives; retire and enjoy life. Someone said "Life is what happens while you are making other plans". Suddenly we were in the limelight. Not because of something we had done, but because of what happened to Jesse and to us.

This was something we had never bargained for. The media people were polite, and professional. We were deer in the headlamps and they treated us with care and compassion. They had their vans parked in single file and they waited patiently for their turn to speak with us.

Note: Various members of the media reported Jesse's age at the time he disappeared, as anywhere from 19-23. Small favor for us, he was actually 19, which meant he could be listed with the National center for Missing and Exploited children. Of course we would know nothing of this until later.

Jesse's school did make contact; They offered to help in anyway they could. We were too numb to say anything but 'thank you'. Later we began to get information that maybe they weren't as helpful as they seemed. Were students asked to keep information from us? Did the Sponsors mislead us when they said they would try to help us meet with students who were with Jesse in Chicago?

Headline 11/27/2006

The *Cumulus/KC* a publication of the communications chain that owned *The Vibe*, radio station where Jesse worked, stated "Jock MIA in Chicago".

Allbusiness.com/radio-monitor reported on Nov 28th, "Sidekick for Shorty and the Boyz, gone missing. This is significant as an example of one of the many different genres in which Jesse played a part.

Note: while looking through notes and article collected through the years, I came across this hardcopy of a site called Missouriolx.com; Someone had left this post: '*hi he is in this country, Kashif-Sultan@hotmail. com* 'A would be psychic? Someone involved in the crime? I had overlooked this piece of information until I started this book. Now I will send it to police(I may have already but can't remember). I just mailed a postcard to Chicago Police with this information on it. We have about 3 years of old articles, and documents about Jesse; It seemed too many to review but since we have some

**additional information from others maybe we can find
something of interest. But I get ahead of myself.**

Headline 12-5-2006: College Students roundup reward

We did learn that Jesse's fraternity, *Lambda Chi Alpha*
was charged with helping raise reward funds, Jesse's fraternity
put together an event(*Opiefest*). They printed t-shirts, sold
them as a fundraiser; they gathered in a room on campus
with friends and family to talk about Jesse. Donna was still
under the weather at that time, so Andy, the Deacon, and
I attended. It was a moving event. I missed some of the
speakers, as the media was there and I didn't want to miss a
chance to spread Jesse's story. Oh to be two places at once.
This event generated about 1300 dollars for the reward
fund. In time the reward would be increased to 4000, then
10,000 dollars.

Funds for the reward came from our employers, our
church, my union, and many caring individuals. I did
make some contacts with Jesse's Frat brothers that would
last until this day. *Opiefest* would morph into an awareness/
fundraising event that would bring in our Church, friends
and family, strangers, new friends, three bands, and good
food, on an annual basis

The name *Opiefest* came from Jesse's character name on
a local radio station which was Opie Cunningham, taken
from two popular Ron Howard characters, Opie Taylor and
Richie Cunningham. Jesse was part of the morning crew
called *Shorty and the Boyz*, on *95.7 the Vibe*, a very popular
Kansas City station.

Around this time period, I began to wander over the
World Wide Web, searching for anything that might relate
to Jesse. I believe there were about 30 pages of information.
Jesse was national news. We heard from people thru

the internet, from all over. I had contact with a woman in Australia; On *Yahoo.com a* woman of Greek descent contacted a friend who had a missing network in Europe and Jesse was added there. I went to *Yahoo*, the French and Spanish versions, and shared his story with English speaking users in French and Spanish speaking countries. This became an obsession with me. We made contact around this time with a wonderful lady in Chicago. Jennifer Long took her children and passed out flyers of Jesse around downtown Chicago, talking to the homeless, hoping to find some lead for us. We would meet her in person on a subsequent trip to Chicago; what a beautiful lady.

The headlines on November 27th contained the following message, concerning Jesse's story: **Police say 'No foul play suspected'**. Donna and I knew better, nothing but foul play would keep our son away from us. We could not imagine what police were thinking if this wasn't foul play. Could the fact they had very little evidence, or clues and that their witnesses were scattered throughout the 50 states, have influenced their statement? It is very difficult not to be paranoid when your dear, sweet son is missing.

Additional headlines on the 28th read, **Deejays ask for help**. The deejays *from 95.7 the Vibe* were asking for any help they could get from listeners. They shared Jesse's story with friends and colleagues in the trade.

November was moving on. Thanksgiving came; We debated going to Donna's family gathering, as we usually did. We did not want to burden the entire family with our sorrows; But in the end we knew we could not just sit at home. It was the right call, Everyone was so great, just being there when we needed them without hanging over us.

No doubt due to so much stress, Donna had a cold and I think a fearful dread of Chicago. I was ready to go, in hopes of some breaking news. Police advised us not to come, the weather was terrible; It was so bad nationwide, that we were supposed to talk with a national news show about Jesse but they called and said they would be doing stories about the weather instead. We hated thinking the weather was more important than Jesse, but it gave us some perspective on what it is like to be a family of the missing. Not everyone is going to think the world has ended.

Finally December came. On December 8th, Deacon Ken Albers, Andy, and myself headed to Chicago. It was bitterly cold. We met with police, and stayed in the Sheraton Inn Office and Towers where Jesse disappeared.

The ghost of his absence haunted the hotel, even as individuals and families swarmed over the building enthused by the holiday decorations and general good cheer. I thought of that old song lyric *"Don't they know it's the end of the world?"*. I had to remind myself that this was a family affair not a world affair. We met with police at the Belmont station. They arranged a press conference and we managed to stumble through the questions. As in Belton, the members of the press were thoughtful and polite. I remember as we were leaving the conference, the local Hispanic station showed up and a man asked me questions and then translated my answers into Spanish for the attractive lady reporter who was in front of the camera. Later Deacon Ken, a truly resourceful man, located the various channels that would be presenting our press conference—including the Hispanic channel. I fielded questions in a slightly unfamiliar voice and perfect Spanish. At this time I also submitted a DNA sample at the request of the police.

Next morning we attended Mass. If we had been more with it we would have spoken to the Priest, but I was ready to return to the quiet of the hotel room. Later we decided to go out in front of the hotel and pass out posters.

Just as we started to leave, my cell rang. It was Sergeant R. He advised us that they had just found a body in the East river just behind the hotel. He wanted us to stay in the hotel so we would not get swarmed by the press. We returned to our rooms and waited. My heart and mind kept saying to me, "don't' think about it, don't' think about what if . . . ." Maybe 15 minutes later, (maybe a day or a week it seemed), Detective R called back. They had a body . . . . but it was not Jesse. This individual had identification and this was apparently a suicide.

We then went out in front of the hotel, in the cold darkness, amid blowing snow, and handed out flyers. People were not very receptive. I know that there are all manner of persons with all manner of causes. When we were able to explain, they took the fliers, some expressing sympathy; Again not the world's problem but ours. We were in Chicago from the 8th until the 10th.

We also learned on this trip that Matthew S, a businessman from East Longmeadow, MA, had disappeared in December of 2005 from the Same hotel where Jesse had gone missing, while attending a business conference. His body was later found in the East river that runs just behind the hotel. I found a site online where his mother-in-law had posted a message. She had seen our story and wanted to talk to us. I was able to locate a number online in Longmeadow, MA for the name S and I was actually able to talk with his wife. She said the police ruled an accident; she wasn't so sure, but could not bear the pain of digging any further. she seemed so vulnerable. I said I understood and that was that.

During this time period apparently there were 20 detectives searching the area. There would be helicopters and boats searching the shoreline; Divers and sonar in the river. Cadaver dogs searched in the area around the hotel and in the streets in 'underground Chicago'. (Apparently there is an area of streets below the streets). Many homeless people call this area home.

Videos were watched, from the hotel and surrounding businesses. There were no results. We were told 100 people were interviewed. As I mentioned earlier, we were troubled by the fact that Jesse's thing's had been gathered and sent home. The hotel rooms were all cleaned and prepared for new business. There was no crime scene and the police were not even calling this a crime. One thing we did know Jesse would never have left of his own accord. He had a newly completed room of his own in the basement (at his request). He was returning to a promotion from unpaid intern to paid employee at the radio station. He had another job to return to, and he was looking at the classes for the next session at UMKC. He might not have said it, but he was missing mom. He always kept in contact with her.

While in Chicago, the hotel charged us nothing for our stay or expenses. They were so polite, I don't think they realized how grateful we were for this show of kindness. Instead of worrying that some one would say "Oh they must feel guilty", they chose to treat us with kindness and compassion. The police worked with AT&T in Chicago. AT&T in Chicago did take posters and have their employees distribute them; and they paid for cab fares during our stay.

Headlines:

12/18/2006 *David Lohr*, crime reporter states '*No Clues*' in reference to Jesse's case

12-27-2006 *Family relies on faith.*

This headline was based on the fact that in almost all our interviews, we shared the strength that our faith and our church family was bringing to us. We could not have stood against such a terrible thing without that faith.

This is as good a point as any to talk about our Church. From the beginning of this terrible event, we were in contact with our Deacon, who kept us in contact with our parish family. You would think that we would have been in Church every Sunday looking for support and strength. The truth is, we could not bear to look at the church, sitting next to the grade school, sitting next to the high school; A 1000 memories and reminders of our son waiting to tear us apart. This was a great dilemma for us. We wanted to be with our church family, even though they too were reminders. But we still craved their love and support. The problem we faced was the minefield of bittersweet places and faces that seemed to speak Jesse's name anytime we got near them.

We were finally able to summon the courage to attend Mass. There were tears during and after the service as we talked with friends. One of these friends, Kevin K, a dear family friend, would Sunday after Sunday rise from his seat and shake hands and give hugs. He and his wife Mary were raising 9 children. An amazing man with a great work ethic, Kevin's house full of redheads, was the perfect place for Jesse in his youth; He blended right in. Kevin was Jesse's soccer coach and sort of surrogate father. He made a special point to give hugs and handshakes to Donna and I after Jesse disappeared.

One day I was surfing the internet, for Jesse related items; I was on *Facebook*. Someone from our church was asking about a recent death within our Parish. I saw a name: Kevin K! How could this be?

It was like God was pitching strike two. Kevin was in his 50's; apparently he had some old issues with his heart. An operation was scheduled. Something went wrong. Times like this we had trouble with our faith. Our son gone, Kevin's family left to fend on their own. I can only say we are still here, fighting the good fight, and so are the K's. The church family came together for us and for the K's. Not to mention the fact that this wonderful family reflected the tremendous determination of Kevin. I am sure they had some doubtful moments as we did, but they too fought the good fight.

There are critics of the Christian faith, the Catholic faith. I can only say it sustains my family. There are no cowards in the true faith, whatever name you give it.

CHAPTER 2

2007

We had some experience early on with purported psychics. A friend referred us to a 'psychic' friend, who was kind but not really helpful. This friendly amateur advised us Jesse was in the Detroit area, on some small island that was at one time an amusement park. We actually sent flyers to the police dept. in that area and they very nicely agreed that they would check into it. Nothing came of that.

Then some unidentified person sent Jesse's name to a 'dream' site. On this site there is a picture of a young wholesome-looking man and his family. He purports to take a name and to dream and tell the family associated with that name, details of the fate of their loved one. Of course there was a fee involved. We refused to pay, but in time he did get around to Jesse's name. He advised us Jesse had met two men, they worked in a garage. There was a dispute over money owed for car repairs, and these men may have been responsible for Jesse's disappearance. Some time later this man called he wanted to start a campaign along with his associate, a famous televison psychic, to distribute posters and begin a search for Jesse. We talked to a friend of ours who had some very negative experiences with so-called psychics. She had heard of this duo and they apparently would contact a family of the missing and get a list of family and friends. They would then use the family to squeeze money from these caring individuals, for the purpose of paying expenses for their television and related operations. We declined the offer. It is a terrible thing that these people would take money this way, but even worse is the torment for the family of the missing one. To get all these false hopes, and these despicable persons never had any intention of helping. We had contact with various individuals with all sorts of information to share. I can only sum up our experience by saying this: "If you are a psychic, go find our son, the reward will be waiting". I have found them to be sympathetically unhelpful to harmful and even deceitful and greedy. Additional advice to families of the missing, If you get some offer for help from a psychic, do not let your grief and sorrow cloud your judgment. Save your resources for more practical activities. I don't need to be psychic to tell you, that most likely you will get burned.

One of the more practical alternatives is the *National Center For Missing and Exploited Children.* Police will probably not tell you this but one of their responsibilities, is to point you to resources such as NCMEC. They can offer advise, get poster's distributed, and be a source of strength. The police working an individual case must initiate contact with the NCMEC.

We can not as families of the missing. NCMEC is primarily for cases of missing children; However we learned there is a federal law that allows anyone, (I believe it's 21), or younger at the time they go missing, to be listed in the missing children's database and to have access to their services. We discovered NCMEC thru another agency, *Project Jason* out of Omaha Nebraska.

March of 2007, Donna, Andy, Deacon Ken and I went to Chicago. We mostly walked the streets following Jesse's trail. We stayed at the Office and Towers. I know Donna and I both had this hope that we would turn a corner and Jesse would be there. We had the good fortune to meet with Jennifer Long, our new friend and supporter in Chicago. We had a nice lunch and she escorted us through the streets of underground Chicago, just off of Michigan Ave. We talked with her and learned about this area. She was a friendly face among the strangers of Chicago. Police declined to see us, something about a shooting and a parade. Donna was disappointed, she had so many questions. I think is was very hard for both of us returning to Belton empty-handed. This was Donna's first trip to Chicago and she would not return for some time.

Kelly Jolkowski is mother to Jason Jolkowski, who disappeared from Omaha, NE on Wednesday, June 13, 2001. Kelly founded *Project Jason* and has been a major force in the movement to help missing families; to promote legislation to give those families a better chance of finding their loved ones; to educate and aid Law Enforcement in their role in the recovery process and the prosecution of guilty parties.

We discovered Kelly on the internet and our whole world changed. We were no longer stumbling in the dark, but we were able to actively participate in the search for our son.

Additionally we learned that we were not alone; that we could reach out to others, to get a helping hand and to lend one. Take some time to go to the internet and research Kelly and her organization, you might find you have something to offer to families of the missing or that they have something to offer to you. You might also learn how to avoid becoming a family of the missing yourself. ***It can happen to anyone.***

Speaking of resources, there is a National Database called *NamUs*. It contains valuable information on the missing, and unidentified victims as well. Comparisons of unidentified individuals, living or deceased and known missing individuals can be made.

Imagine finding your loved one in an unmarked grave or lying in a hospital bed somewhere. The thought of your loved one being out there and never knowing what happened is excruciating. If families of the missing, law enforcement, hospitals, and medical examiners took advantage of this tool, many families with missing loved ones could find answers to some of the most important questions in their lives.

Through *Project Jason* our son Jesse was featured in a Trucker's magazine. A group called *18 Wheel Angels* works with *Project Jason*. They are like a posse, looking for your loved ones and leaving copies of their magazine at truck stops across the nation. This was where one of our few potential sightings originated. Apparently a truck driver in Texas thought he saw someone like Jesse. Police in Texas checked and reported to Chicago police. No sign of Jesse was found but we at least knew someone was looking. We also had a report from a Canadian gentleman who contacted police, when he saw an ad on *Craigslist*, and the picture with the ad looked much like Jesse. Again it was a false alarm.

We submitted the following information to the *18 Wheel Angels* magazine.

18 Wheel Angels

Jesse Warren Ross

Jesse Warren Ross
Classification: Endangered Missing Adult
Alias / Nickname: Opie
Date of Birth: February 18, 1987
Date Missing: November 21, 2006
From City/State: Chicago, IL
Age at Time of Disappearance: 19
Gender: Male **Race:** White
Height: 70 inches **Weight:** 140 pounds
Hair Color: Red **Eye Color:** Blue
Complexion: Light
Glasses/Contacts Description: Glasses with dark wire frames.
Identifying Characteristics: Freckles.
Clothing: White T-shirt, green warm-up jacket, blue jeans, black athletic shoes.

Circumstances of Disappearance: Unknown. Jesse was last seen at approximately 2:30am leaving a meeting at a hotel in the vicinity of the 300 block of E. North Water St. in Chicago, IL.
Investigative Agency: Chicago Police

Department
Phone: (312) 744-8266
Investigative Case #: HM-733282

Jesse is Project Jason's 18 Wheel Angel Poster Campaign for June 1-15. Please visit our website, and download and distribute his poster, located at http://www.projectjason.org/18wheel.html.

Jesse Ross
by Don, Donna, and Andy Ross

Jesse Warren Ross, DOB: 02/18/1987, Height: 5' 10", Weight: 140 lbs, with red hair, blue eyes, and freckles, last seen Nov 21, 2006 wearing a green jacket, white t-shirt, blue jeans and black jogging shoes. Currently there is a $10,000 reward for information leading to his return. People are asked to call Chicago Police at 312-744-8266.

Jesse left his home in Belton MO, on Nov 18, 2006 to go to Chicago for 4 days as part of a Model United Nations event with the University of Missouri, Kansas City. On Nov 21, at approximately 2:00 am Jesse attended a simulated security council meeting with a partner at the Sheraton Towers hotel on Water Street. Around 3:00 am Jesse left the conference room on a break; he was believed to be going back to his hotel, the Sheraton Four Points hotel off of Michigan Ave, a 10 minute walk. He hasn't been seen since leaving the meeting room.

Jesse is an outgoing, charming individual. He majors in Communications and minors in Politics. As a youth, he played soccer and was involved in scouting. In high school he was involved in Cross Country, track, yearbook staff, and Knowledge Bowl. At UMKC, he was involved in a number of student organizations, and was pledging a fraternity. He had an internship at a local radio station that was about to become a paid position as part of the morning show (Shorty and the Boys at 95.7 The Vibe in Kansas City). He was working for a Voice Over Internet company as well, and was looking forward to his next school term.

At this time, the Chicago Police have no leads in this case. We have been working to spread Jesse's story nationwide, as there is no telling where we may get a clue. Jesse's vibrant personality and big heart have left a huge vacancy for his family and friends.

We all just want him home.

―――――

Peter D is a private investigator who has offices here around Belton. Someone suggested a PI might be helpful so I began to search the internet and found Peter's services. I called and left a message. He was out of the country at the time but promised to get back to me. He did and I shared Jesse's story. He asked to have time to go over Jesse's information and to get back. He did. This is the beginning of a story of gaining a friend, a very special friend with resources and skills we were sadly lacking. I want to quickly point out, Peter worked with us from a personal interest in Jesse's case. We could not afford to put a full time PI on Jesse's case, as it is with many families. We want to point out that Peter is a professional; He makes a living searching and compiling facts for people. Occasionally someone in his field can do some 'Pro Bono' work, charging a minimal fee, but he cannot be expected to simply abandon his living and pursue all our problems. We would recommend to families of the missing to seek out someone who might be able to volunteer time or work for a small fee. We all work for a living and we get paid for our services. That is how we survive. Same here. Certainly our loss is of paramount importance to us, but we can't expect the whole world to stop spinning.

Just saying this, Peter performed a number of critical services for us, actually getting results when the police said "**You** need to take care of this". Police will not allow any outsider, including family, to interfere with their investigation, even when the investigation hasn't moved in 4 years. Just saying again, don't expect miracles, but an individual like Peter is a blessing.

In January of 2007, one of Donnas' close friends and his fiancee went to Chicago to handout posters about Jesse. They were on the news that year. We can never thank them enough. I think we were still in shock and unable to put all this together at the time.

FYI, on February 12th, 2007, We registered Jesse with an online site for the missing. missingperson@crimstopperswanted.com

A parent from our boys' High School had connections in Chicago regarding 2 full-sized billboards featuring Jesse's case. They were to be placed on 2 major highways around Chicago. Seeing these billboards was the main reason that Donna was going to Chicago. Police agreed to drive us by the billboards, but a shooting and another crime took priority over us and so we never got to see the billboards.

KARA KOPETSKY IS MISSING. THIS IS A PICTURE OF HER ABOVE. IF YOU HAVE SEEN OR HAVE ANY INFORMATION ABOUT HER PLEASE CONTACT THE POLICE OR CALL (816) 689-4199, (816) 217-2064 OR (816) 985-8636. KARA IS 5'5 125 POUNDS WITH LIGHT HAIR AND HAZEL EYES. HER FAMILY AND FRIENDS ARE VERY WORRIED ABOUT HER. PLEASE HELP US BY REPOSTING THIS PICTURE.

The old silent movies would show a sign saying "Meanwhile back at the ranch', Well meanwhile back in Belton, 17 year old Kara Kopetsky went missing in May of 2007. She disappeared from her high school.

Kara's family was desperate. Her stepfather James Beckford went door to door handing out flyers. He happened to stop at the home of My wife's sister, Debbie. She referred him to us. Since that time, we have shared some sorrow, some laughter, awareness events, and Mexican food at *Mi Pueblito*. This is a wonderful family and it is easier to bear our burden when we think of this family and their burden. They have been so generous in their support of our cause.

Opiefest 2 took place in downtown Kansas City. A band called *A Dead Giveaway* had taken part in Jesse's senior project at O'Hara high school; A battle of the bands fundraiser Jesse organized for Catholic Charities in January of 2005, Called *Rock Against Hunger*; it raised around $600.00. The band wanted to do a benefit for Jesse. We traveled to the *El Torreon* ballroom on May 2007 and listened to the band and others play for Jesse. Friends and family were there, but it was a small gathering. Not great in numbers, but the spirit was there.

The first fundraising/awareness event took place at UMKC; we had little to do with that also. This first event later was dubbed *Opiefest*. *Opiefest 2* was the real beginning of a future legacy involving Our family, the band, and a host of enthusiastic volunteers.

The band did all the organizing for Opiefest 2. Donna and I were novices to the whole concept of fundraising and awareness planning. Like I said it was a small event, but the media was present and we along with members of the bands

 family, were interviewed. We received a call from one of the local stations. They had not been notified and expressed their willingness to carry Jesse's story. We began to see that there was a great deal to know about event planning.

On June 13th, 2007, it was the sixth anniversary of the disappearance of Jason Jolkowsky in Omaha. Omaha Mayor Mike Fahey had declared that day as Omaha Missing Person's day. Project Jason and founder Kelly Jolkowski, Jason's mother, were having an event to commemorate the day. The CUE center, a non-profit organization from North Carolina led by founder Monica Caison, was stopping in Omaha for this event. The CUE center provides searches and assistance for families of the missing.

Donna and I had become acquainted with Kelly online and we were one of the families to be recognized at this event. There was music and prayer. I remember we processed into the church where the event was held, as an Air Force Color Guard with bagpipes preceded us. Our Jesse, Jason, and Erin Popisil, who disappeared at age 15, on June 3rd, 2001 were featured missing. Also Singer-songwriter Gina Bos who disappeared on October 17th, 2000 after performing at a pub in Lincoln Nebraska was included amongst the missing to be honored. Lastly, 18 year old Jackie Rains-Kracman, who had been missing for nearly 42 years, at the time, was another name on the list of honorees. This event was a real eye-opener for us. We saw first hand that we were not alone. We had the opportunity to visit with the other families present. It was much like staring into a mirror, finally seeing what we must look like to others. It was also like discovering that angels are real and actually are among us(*Angels among us*—Alabama)

In September of 2007, we sent out emails, asking people to send postcards to the Chicago Mayor's office to ask about the lack of progress on Jesse's case. Donna's sister wrote an impassioned letter to the Mayor. Apparently it was a very good letter. We were contacted by phone by Chicago police trying to get into contact with Donna's sister, Susan. On September 19, the mayor's office drafted a letter to Susan. Among the assurances within the text of that letter, it stated "that Missing Person Supervising Sergeant Tony R has been in contact with their private investigator". What the letter didn't say is that the PI was informed he could not participate in an open investigation; Nor could any other agency. At this time Jesse's case had been cold just short of a year. Some of you may think that 11 months seems a short time to be writing the Mayor's office, but if you think about it, one day of not knowing the whereabouts of someone you love is an eternity. As I have said before, I don't think anyone, police, Mayor, whatever, would be content with this situation if it were their child. And this was just the beginning. As time moved on, the case became colder and colder, yet remained just as 'active' to those charged with finding our son.

On November 7[th,] 2007 we had a church service at St. John Francis Church, our parish. Friends gathered to remember Jesse and to say prayers for his safe return We deeply appreciated the thought and memories shared by all.

We travelled to Chicago again in Nov 2007. This was a very busy time for us. Myself and Deacon Ken Albers (pictured above) again stayed at the Sheraton office and towers on Water street. This trip we met in Chicago with Marcus Moore, a reporter from the Kansas City area, who had done previous stories on Jesse. He followed us on our sojourn through the city. Also at this time, for the first time we were allowed to tour the hotel with members of the Chicago media, along with a Private Investigator we were working with from Chicago. We were able to trace Jesse's actual steps up to the time of the meeting, to see the various exits, and the room where he was last seen. One of Jesse's sponsors, D, was present for the current session of the mock UN conference going on. This certainly gave me a sense of unease, thinking of the young men and women present at that time; potential victims of Jesse's fate? D told us that there had been a meeting before the session began, a sharing of Jesse's story and a caution to all. This same year there was a special page in the handout for attendees also with Jesse's story featured. We had extensive coverage during this trip. It was suggested for the media that Jesse had some secret life, and was maybe hiding out? There was no evidence to suggest any of this and I think it was a ploy to sensationalize. After a busy day we returned to the hotel and then went for pizza with some of Jesse's old friends who lived in the area. Again we took care of Jesse business, but made sure we took care of ourselves as well. I learned some of the activities behind a news presentation; Walking down a street a number of times until the camera shot was right.; Ignoring some overzealous bystanders who wanted to join me in the shot. The media is a powerful tool in our quest, but it is a business and we give some to them so they give to us. This is not a condemnation, but a statement of reality.

During this trip, we notified police we were in the city. They were very eager for a meeting. Deacon Ken, the Chicago PI, and myself met with a large number of detectives and the Lt. in charge. They were very aggressive and unhappy that I had apparently told the press they were no longer working Jesse's case. It was almost like a mass interrogation. I understood their annoyance, but the fact is I didn't tell anyone they were backing off on Jesse's case. That information came from a Chicago newspaper. Donna and I had some feelings about this but we never talked to the press about them. Some of the detectives were suggesting that we were impeding their investigation by our failure to get certain things done. Donna and I were under the apparently mistaken impression that the police were responsible for such things as DNA, fingerprints, etc.

Maybe we have watched too many police shows; had developed some unreal expectations of what police really do. At any rate, we talked things out and left with everyone smiling. I knew that getting angry would not help Jesse's case and that from a police perspective they certainly were under the gun to produce some results. They assured me that they were working Jesse's case and would pursue any leads that might come up. I remembered the sympathetic help we received from all the detectives when we first travelled to Chicago and I sensed the frustration at having no leads. Donna and I still are impatient for some results, but we do not blame police for Jesse's disappearance; we blame those who actually took him from us, and we continue to believe beyond doubt that someone has done just that.

CHAPTER 3
2008

In May of 2008, I decided I would travel to Chicago at some time when there wasn't snow on the ground, and a cold wind blowing in from the lake. So I contacted our PI, Peter and proposed we make the journey. Donna's opinion of Chicago has never changed, she still dislikes the city, and I understand that; she just wants to bring Jesse home. That's probably not going to happen anytime soon, but I feel the determination to go as much as she feels the need to stay. Peter is not fond of flying, so we decided to take the Amtrak train from Kansas City to Chicago. It did have the advantage of arriving at O'Hare airport right next to our hotel. I can only say 8 hours on Amtrak was not my idea of heaven, but it got us there. At least they didn't strip search us getting on and off the train. Also on this trip, I became aware of the rail system in Chicago. We were able to get a pass for 3 days of riding anywhere we could want to go in Chicago. In all my previous trips we travelled mostly by foot, occasionally by taxi; sometimes through the courtesy of the Chicago Police.

When we arrived in Chicago, we checked into the hotel. Our hotel was close to the Airport, so it was very nice. We rode the rails and visited various places. Peter and I split up at the hotel (Sheraton Inn) where Jesse had disappeared and he followed some leads. He took pictures of the video cameras on various buildings and at intersections in the area around the Sheraton Inn. He found out at this time that Chicago hired a company to clean graffiti from the various structures within the city, (Smiley face murders referred to elsewhere in this book).

We contacted the police. They agreed to meet and take us to lunch. We met with Detective Tim O. Peter talked with him concerning the case and what we had been doing and learning since our arrival. Maybe I am getting paranoid but I sensed that the lunch was perhaps a diversion to keep us at a distance from the files and resources that they would most assuredly keep Peter from accessing. Detective O had been assigned Jesse's case while Detective R the original lead on the case, was on medical leave. He took many notes and seemed unfamiliar with Jesse's case. He informed us that he was actually assigned to the financial fraud division, and had worked the financial aspects of Jesse's case. Neither Peter nor I felt really warm and fuzzy after our time with Detective O. He did seem sympathetic to our situation, I have to say that.

On this trip we also stopped at the Sheraton Inn-Four Points, where Jesse had been staying during the conference. They seemed reluctant to talk with us, and we left with little in the way of contact.

In May, Chicago is truly a beautiful sight for tourists; boats moving up and down the East river; people in the parks, and on the lake. The rail system was very clean and actually impressive.

We did have to ride a bus when a section of the track was under repair, but it was still the best way to get around town. It may seem strange to hear me speak nicely about the city that swallowed up my son. I do not hold the city of Chicago responsible for what happened to Jesse. I hold those who may have harmed him, responsible. And I hold the police responsible for seeking out the truth and giving us some kind of peace.

We boarded the Amtrak train for the trip home. I was putting heavy bags in the overhead and had the misfortune to tear both rotator cuffs. This would later lead to two surgeries to correct the problem. Despite the excellent weather and the festive nature of Chicago in May, I did not find this trip all that fulfilling. I don't mind going to

Chicago, but like Donna, there is a part of me that wants to culminate the trip by bringing Jesse home. There is a certain amount of disappointment in each trip when this does not happen.

June 1st, 2008, I received a bulletin from Project Jason. It concerned an awareness opportunity with an internet site called Second Life. Second Life is a virtual reality world. This popular site, with over one million members, might have as many as 40,000+ people signed on at any given time. Denise Harrison is the creative genius behind this endeavor. You may ask how this affects families of the missing. Well within this virtual world, of color and dimension, there is a site called the Garden for the Missing. A registered member (no charge by the way) may explore this virtual world and see posters of the missing, in a beautiful setting of sand, beach, and building. It is possible to access written stories of each missing, and one may interact with others living persons, each represented by an impressively crafted Avatar(an animated character representing a real online user). It is also possible to link to the Project Jason forum, to see detailed information about each missing person that is featured, by simply clicking on a poster. Over the years, Denise has expanded the site; It has a meeting room for real time meetings. There is a beach; one can even ride a jet ski, (If you are more coordinated than I am.) Denise is usually on hand, or no more than a message away, if you get lost. We are proud to have Jesse featured on this site.

Somewhere in 2008, I believe, I stumbled upon a site called *Peace4themissing*. Not a non-profit, or a for-profit, but a small group of individuals dedicated to helping with a variety of causes; Missing persons, domestic violence, and child abuse to mention a few. A sympathetic person called Sara offered help to us as well as many others in need. Over the years we have called upon her and her associates in helping to promote Jesse's cause, and to help us reach out to help others. I became an admin for Justice4 the Justified, a spinoff of Peace4. Sara and company goes beyond definition. They maintain a flexibility that allows this organization to reach out to many, as long as there is a need.

On the Road to Remember tour (August or September 2008), CUE is an organization for the missing out of North Carolina. They came to our home to feature Jesse and to the homes of various families of the missing in Missouri and other states. They assist families of the missing by traveling the country organizing, performing searches, and awareness events. Monica Caison founder and director of CUE brought her staff and resources to our home. Also featured was Kara Kopetsky, missing from Belton in May 2007. Monica created this event, and made it the success it was. We were thrilled to see many old friends and family from out of town. The event culminated in a balloon release, which was dignified and moving to all present. Media was present also. As impressive as this all was, we were only one stop of many in this epic journey of hope on the part of Monica and company. Groups like CUE may be the only hope for many families with missing.

Flyer for Cue tour:

In support of missing children **CUE Center For Missing Persons**

P.O. Box 12714
Wilmington, N.C. 28411
(910) 343-1131
www.ncmissingpersons.org

Contact:
Monica Caison
(910) 232-1687
cuecenter@aol.com

For immediate release

National Tour Visits Missouri to Revive Missing Persons Cases
Advocates Are Traveling Cross-Country in the 5ᵗʰ Annual "On the Road to Remember" Tour

Missouri—RALLY STOPS

• **Family & Friends of Missing—Branson Perry**

Wilmington, NC—For the fifth year, volunteers from the North Carolina-based CUE Center for Missing Persons will set out on another cross country tour to raise awareness of missing children and adults. The team is scheduled to make numerous appearances throughout Missouri in August; distributing a trail of DVD's, press kits and valuable information concerning 110 missing persons and 6 unsolved homicide cases. Many Missouri cases are included in this year's tour and several will be highlighted at the groups pre planned rally stops that will include participation from law enforcement agencies, advocates—organizations, families of the missing and local and state officials.

"After so many years, missing persons and homicide cases fade from the public's radar, but for the families and friends left behind, the nightmare continues—every minute of every day," said CUE Founder, Monica Caison, who is leading the caravan of volunteers". "We make this trip each year to assure no case fades from memory and to support the families who remain searching for a resolution. They need our help and the community's help to bring forth information."

The 2008 tour, On the Road to Remember will depart from Wilmington, NC on August 21st, and will end more than 5, 299 miles later returning the volunteers to their home state North Carolina, on September 2nd. Hundreds of volunteers will take part in various legs of the tour, which will include thirty rally stops, traveling thru seventeen states in an effort to promote a public awareness.

- **Family of Missing—Jeremy Alex (Grand Rally Honoree Stop)**

Tom Watkins Park 2100 West High Springfield, Missouri 65803

- **Family of Missing—Bianca Noel Piper**

(Intersection) McIntosh Hill Road & Hwy 79 Foley, Missouri 63347

- **Family of Missing—Amanda Jones**

Jefferson County Sheriff Office 510 1st Street Hillsboro, Missouri 63050

14635 Ember Road Craig, Missouri 64437
- **Families of Missing—Kara Kopetsky & Jesse Ross**

Residence 15706 Lawrence Avenue Belton, Missouri 64012

For a complete tour schedule visit CUE's website and click on the Road Tour button; www.ncmissingpersons.org

# # #

National Tour Purpose and Inspiration

The annual tour was created to generate new interest in cold cases of missing people across our nation. The inspiration came in 2004 from the case of North Carolina college student Leah Roberts, who had gone on a cross-country trip of self-exploration. Her wrecked and abandoned vehicle was found, but Leah is still missing. Leah's case went cold and interest faded until CUE volunteers set out on a grueling 14-day trip to retrace her route and inform the media of all those who were missing in the path of the tour. In the years to follow, it only seemed right to keep hope alive after families across the country voiced the need for more help and supported the tour.

National Tour Objective

The national road tour, called "On the Road to Remember," is an awareness campaign that focuses on missing persons cases that have gone cold or have not received appropriate media coverage on the local level—much less the national level. The tour, which travels through many states annually, provides that attention.

In all cases of missing people, it is vital to inform the public of the missing person's circumstances quickly and to disseminate that information to the media and the public. In most cases where details are released immediately to the public through an organized campaign, the public brings forth information that aids in the investigation and or the location of the victim. The media plays a significant role in getting the word out on the behalf of the missing person and should be recognized as a vital resource to any investigation.

Interest in many of the cases we have featured in previous tours has been renewed. The media has learned about local cases they were unaware of; case investigations have been renewed, and searches conducted. Information has resulted in new leads in some cases, and has even helped identify an unknown decedent. And finally, some of the missing have been found, which is the main reason we conduct the tour every year, despite the toll it takes on our all-volunteer staff.

It is the belief of the CUE Center for Missing Persons that all investigations, the public, volunteers and the media should work in collaboration on cases involving missing children and adults; until this happens, there will continue to be cases of the missing labeled "cold" or "inactive."

About CUE

Founded in 1994, the non-profit CUE Center, based in Wilmington, N.C., provides support, services and search efforts to families of the missing. To date, CUE has assisted more than 8,200 families in need. CUE is entirely supported by donations and active volunteers.

About Monica Caison

Exposed to families suffering a missing person three times before the age of 25, Monica Caison decided take action. In 1994, she founded the CUE Center for Missing Persons, which provides assistance for those who have lost a loved one, utilizing media contacts, conducting extensive searches, and going to any length necessary to locate missing persons, regardless of their age, race, sex or socio-economic background. CUE picks up where law enforcement leaves off.

Mrs. Caison has received numerous local, state and national awards for her volunteerism and tireless spirit. As a fulltime volunteer, Mrs. Caison is driven to help restore the faith in humanity that family members inevitably lose knowing that someone, somewhere, knows what happened to their missing loved one.

National Tour—Quick Facts

- Rally Stops—30
- States Traveling Through—17
- Cases Missing Featured—110
- Case Homicide Featured—6
- Miles Traveled Total—5,299

For full tour dates and location, as well as a complete listing of cases featured on the tour, e-mail <u>cuecenter@aol.com</u> or call Monica Caison at (910) 343-1131 or 24 Hour Line (910) 232-1687.

In September of 2008 we traveled to Omaha Nebraska for *Miles for The Missing*, an event sponsored by *Project Jason*. Gathered at lake side, families of the missing, accompanied by supporters and well-wishers, presented stories and then walked or bicycled or pushed strollers around the circumference of the lake. Then we dined on franks and hamburgers. We shared our grieving and our joy for the wonderful people we were meeting for the first time. I especially enjoyed meeting two young boys, they were brothers. They had lost someone, and knew of our Jesse but they couldn't contain the natural enthusiasm of youth, and the feelings were contagious. Again Kelly J. performed a minor miracle.

At the *Miles for The Missing* event we were fortunate to make the acquaintance of a young lady named Christina Fontana. She was attending this event to gather video and first hand interviews with those of us having missing loved ones. This wonderful woman was putting together a documentary about the epidemic of missing in our country; Giving families of the missing the opportunity to share. We would see more of her at the Project Jason retreats in 2009 and 2010.

At this point I will say something about Facebook. We are not directly associated with Facebook. But this has become the primary medium for our contact with the world of the missing. We have established contacts with many individuals and groups through this medium. So I am not speaking for or against this particular social medium;

Just saying it can be a great tool if you are seeking help in contacting those who deal with the missing.

I would also add, that like any other internet resource you need to take precautions when making contacts. FB is a free social network; I don't believe they spend an immense amount of money on sophisticated security measures so be cautious

In November we had *Opiefest 3.* This was our first *Opiefest* at the church. We had the band, *A Dead Giveaway,* and a band called *The Burnt End,* made up of some very talented musicians from our church. We had food, drink and information on the missing, and items for raffling. This would be the format for *Opiefest* celebrations to come.

In December of 2008, Kelly Jolkowski asked member families of Project Jason to share memories with all member families. I created a Christmas letter. The content follows.

Christmas memories

One of my fondest Christmas memories as a boy was going to the Orpheum theatre in Wichita with my dad to see Santa. We also saw Tex Ritter (the late father of the late John Ritter of *Three's a Company* fame). Tex was one of the early singing cowboys, like Gene Autry and Roy Rogers. We received Christmas stockings and the flavor of peppermint candy cane and cream filled chocolate has stayed with me to this very day.

With my own family I remember it was Jesse's job early on to move the little mouse from pocket to pocket on our Christmas calendar, a job he took very seriously. He and Andy would pass out gifts Christmas morn. Jesse would leave Santa cookies and milk, but He would also leave gifts for Santa, a toy truck or car, or a stuffed animal. He would have been hurt if Santa hadn't taken these things, so Santa did. I imagine he recycled them to some needy child somewhere.

Andy in bright pj's and curly blonde hair, rubbing the sleep out of his eyes, was the Christmas poster boy. In contrast to Jesse's burning energy, Andy quietly took in the experience. Andy got his first bicycle for Christmas and it was huge (by little boy standards). Being practical parents we felt he would grow into it and it would last him a long time (parents beware practicality). He accepted it with quiet grace, but I think he would have been justified in saying "Are you nuts? How am I supposed to get on this thing, it's a tank!"

Donna made sure we got to church; she made sure everyone ate a good breakfast. And that every Christmas was a time of love. She also made sure we went to the tree lot and cut down a fresh tree each year. For me this was a love hate relationship. Hauling that tree around in the cold was a pain, but the experience with Donna and the boys was wonderful. We bought hot chocolate for a quarter while they prepared the tree. Andy and Jesse were in charge of the two wheeled cart for transporting the tree thru the lot. I

Remember one Christmas Andy was sitting on the long handles sticking out the front of the cart and Jesse was sitting on the back of the cart. I had cut the tree and said "bring the cart". Andy jumped up and the handles on the cart flew skyward. The back of the cart thudded into the ground and Jesse did a back flip out of the cart. I think he landed on his head, which might explain some things about his behavior in later years.

Andy, Jesse, and I had the job of putting sprinkles on the Christmas cookies Donna would bake. We also had to sample them on a regular basis for quality. Christmas cookies had a short lifespan at our house.

We would drive thru the chill December night to spend Christmas with my family in Wichita, then return to have Christmas with Donna's family. I once wrote a small verse about one of those trips.

Long drive
On a cold December night
The air is clear,
The stars are bright.

At times it seems that someone not only stole our future with Jesse, but the past as well; They took some of the joy from the warm memories. Seems they robbed a whole world of people of the pleasure of Jesse's company. Everything Jesse was, is, and would have been taken. I wrote that short poem, and the picture in my mind was myself driving, Donna sitting next to me and two sweet boys sleeping in the back seat. We will not let any worthless, poor excuse for a human being take that from us. We will keep Jesse and all our memories close to our hearts; And they will warm us on those cold December nights.

CHAPTER 4

2009

On June 12th, We journeyed to Nebraska for the *Project Jason* Retreat for families of the missing. Kelly J. assembled a staff of wellness professionals, with an agenda geared towards healing. We attended a series of sessions covering the many facets of life for families of the missing. Sharing with other families of the missing, that we had yet to know, we learned to grow and to face what might lay ahead for us. Laughing, crying, sharing. We learned that as sad as our story was, it was not necessarily the saddest. We were learning to live our new 'normal' lives

We met at a Christian facility outside of Omaha, with a lake, and beautiful rural surroundings. This was our first introduction to the powers of healing available through *Project Jason* and the staff of caring individuals we were to meet. We learned to put our troubles aside and look at the lives of those around us. Our last night we all gathered in the evening for a casual gathering; S'mores, popcorn, good conversation, these were some of the elements of this evening. We shared our favorite moments from the retreat; Poked some good-hearted fun at some of the awkward moments we all experienced during these healing days. Most importantly, we learned it was alright to laugh, and to feel good from time to time, even in the midst of tragedy. In the movie *Batman Begins,* the father of young Bruce Wayne asks "Why do we fall down? So we can learn to get back up". That's what we were doing, getting back up and learning to live again.

This was the first annual retreat, but not the last for us. By the time we returned home, we had an army of new friends and supporters and we were convinced of the wonderful things Project Jason was capable of. We were especially blessed for the services of Duane Bowers, LPC, an excellent counselor, and friend to families of the missing.

On November 9th, 2009 we had *Opiefest 4* at our church again. Bands, food, raffle items, displays of the missing including Jesse. We were honored to have Kara Kopetsky's family in attendence. This year we also met Ralph Parker, Jesse's friend and roommate from the Chicago event where Jesse disappeared. Ralph and Jesse were partners from UMKC at the mock security council meeting. Ralph was also one of the last persons to see Jesse before he disappeared from the meeting. Note: Ralph was the only person out of 30 or so who ever talked to us. As we heard later that there might have been some who didn't want us talking to students, we began to think this might be the case. We had tried with little success to meet some of those who were with Jesse, but no one wanted to talk to us, even Ralph. He finally agreed to talk with our PI. This was sometime before *Opiefest 4*. I had two short phone conversations with Ralph previously. When he appeared at *Opiefest 4* with other friends of Jesse's this was our first chance to actually see some of Jesse's young friends since he had disappeared. Ralph was warm and very friendly. We did not press him for detailed info about Jesse as we had an event to run.

In 2006, We had built a new bedroom in the basement for Jesse's use, just before he went to Chicago. He was excited to return and paint the walls, red and blue as he was a big fan of KU basketball. He wanted one wall white so his friends could come visit and autograph this wall. (At *Opiefest 4*, we had poster board on the walls and asked people to sign Jesse's 'wall'. Ralph did so). The wall hangs in Jesse's room in the basement; we call it the waiting room waiting for Jesse's return)

In June, some of the band members for *A Dead Giveaway* traveled with me to Chicago. We met up there with friends Steven and Jessica. Steve and Jesse went to high school together. Jessica was Steve's friend. The band and I settled into a Motel in Joliet Illinois. Steve and Jessica hooked up with us later and became invaluable guides during our wanderings in the Windy City. We walked the streets, and stopped in some shops, all the while putting up posters of Jesse. Steve, our most enthusiastic member was seen to actually chase a bus, to tape a poster to the back of it. Kids, do not try this at home!

We all rode the train into Chicago and walked everywhere once we were in the city proper; we found out the Taste of Chicago festival was in progress, so we invaded the festivities.

Breaking up into teams we moved around the site, leaving posters taped everywhere that looked good. We talked with some of the local folks, sharing Jesse's story. We tried to get a place for the band to set up; the guys had brought guitars. Unfortunately this is the big city and the police informed us we could not get a permit at that time and no permit meant no playing. It was still a good experience.

We gathered for lunch, at the hotel where Jesse had disappeared. It was time to do something for ourselves. I was surprised when the band presented me with a certificate, naming a star in the heavens after Jesse. I imagine if there are aliens living out there, they might dispute my claim, but I was thrilled by this wonderful act.

Later we met to take the train back to the motel; During the ride to Joliet, some passengers saw the bands guitars and soon we had a concert going on. Everyone was thrilled, except the conductor who came through a number of times to rain on our parade. One of the passengers was a young man and he gave the conductor so much trouble we began to envision ourselves set off the train; in the dark; somewhere in Chicago, with no transportation. Fortunately that didn't happen. I also had the opportunity to pass out 'Jesse' buttons and to share his story.

When we got back to the hotel, I was tired and went to my room. There was a knock at my door. The band members, Steve, and Jessica appeared. The lights went out I began to wonder what is happening. They had a cake. I then remembered it was my birthday. This is such a wonderful group of young people.

Bryce Veazey with the band was forced to leave early due to a death in the family. On our last day, I decided to take the remaining members of the band into Chicago for some r & r. I drove (help me Lord) into the city all the way up Lakeshore drive up to the Navy Pier. We toured the pier, took a boat following the shoreline and ended up at the museum and Aquarium. It was Sunday so we couldn't get into either. We then walked back along shoreline, to the Navy Pier. We took a lot of pictures, and enjoyed the sunshine and 'people watched'.

I let one of the guys drive and we headed back to the motel. Later I found out that the previous night, the band had talked with the desk person at the hotel and he had a band also. While I was sleeping, there was a party going on. I had promised mother's that I would see that these guys stayed out of trouble; and they did. I love the way they are so unpredictable and fun-loving, like our Jesse, but inside very responsible when it comes to the important issues.

The next day we left for home. We did not have Bryce but we had his GPS. The guys had to pick up some batteries for it and we were on our way. I had great confidence in this group, so I turned my vehicle over to the guys and took a nap.

When I awoke I looked out the window. Nothing was familiar; No wide open landscape, 4 lane highway stretching to infinity. Instead we were on a narrow two lane road surrounded by greenery. The guys had stopped at a cute little country store.

I asked "Where are we? "Hannibal" one of the guys told me. "How did we get here?" I ask again. "Oh we're just following the GPS." Good idea I thought, blame the technology. Actually this was a nice diversion. I met an older couple on a bright red Harley Davidson motorcycle. In talking with them I discovered that there were a limited number of these bikes, dedicated to the firefighters who had perished at 9/11 ground zero. And this particular date, they were all out, attempting to ride a combined total of 1,000,000 miles in memory of these brave firefighters. They told me that they had heard the actual total miles were something like 11,000,000. I decided it was fate, not the GPS that brought us here.

Again in 2009, we journeyed to Omaha for the *Miles for the Missing* event. We saw the same familiar faces and some new ones. Taking in the sunshine, and beautiful lake in the background, we found this to be a great healing event.

CHAPTER 5

2010

Donald Ross

*Jennifer
Hyman*

| Richard M. Daley | Department of Police • City of Chicago | Jody P. Weis |
| Mayor | 35:0 S. Michigan Avenue • Chicago, Illinois 60653 | Superintendent of Police |

April 22, 2010

D.A. Ross
15706 Lawrence Avenue
Belton, MO 64012

Dear Mr. Ross:

We are in receipt of your correspondence which was forwarded to our attention by the Office of the Superintendent. As you know, I recently appeared on Fox News Chicago to discuss your son's case with Mark Saxenmeyer. It is my hope that something new and beneficial will result in the additional media coverage. I mentioned to Mr. Saxenmeyer that I received a postcard from you last May and that I keep it in my office on my bulletin board as a reminder to myself about your son's case. I know that you have all the contact numbers of my Special Victim's Unit staff. Please do not hesitate to contact them if you have any additional concerns, questions or new information. We will continue to follow-up on any leads that become available.

Sincerely,

Commander
Area 3 Detective Division
Chicago Police Department

First letter was from the commander, Area 3, Detective Division.

It was followed by a second letter, prompted by our postcards and petitions sent to the mayor and police representatives.

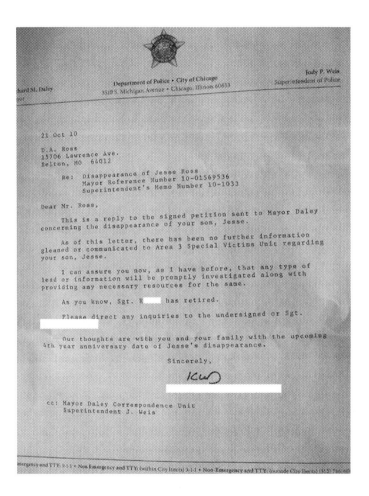

21 Oct 10

D.A. Ross
15706 Lawrence Ave.
Belton, MO 64012

   Re: Disappearance of Jesse Ross
       Mayor Reference Number 10-01569536
       Superintendent's Memo Number 10-1033

Dear Mr. Ross,

    This is a reply to the signed petition sent to Mayor Daley
concerning the disappearance of your son, Jesse.

    As of this letter, there has been no further information
gleaned or communicated to Area 3 Special Victims Unit regarding
your son, Jesse.

    I can assure you now, as I have before, that any type of
lead or information will be promptly investigated along with
providing any necessary resources for the same.

    As you know, Sgt. R███ has retired.

    Please direct any inquiries to the undersigned or Sgt.

    Our thoughts are with you and your family with the upcoming
4th year anniversary date of Jesse's disappearance.

           Sincerely,

cc: Mayor Daley Correspondence Unit
    Superintendent J. Weis

We received these letters from Chicago Police in 2010. They are very nice, business like letter, sympathetic, reassuring. If you are a family of a missing person and you have not seen them or had a clue as to their whereabouts in almost 4 years despite the efforts of the Chicago Police force, this letter means little. I guess in fairness to the police I would say that no family is going to be happy with anything less than success. Can you bring my son home? Then I don't think there is anything else I need from you. I have lots of people to be sympathetic, and reassuring; plenty of folks to commiserate with. I only have one group who needs to bring Jesse home. That is the sound of 4 years of frustration. Police say this an active investigation, and yet nothing has changed in all this time. As an active investigation, it cannot be referred to another agency.

Our PI is forbidden to help with the investigation. I will keep this letter in case one of those investigating should find him/herself in our situation and need some encouragement. Below is a copy of the letter we sent back.

$10,000 REWARD
FOR INFORMATION LEADING TO THE
RETURN OF **JESSE ROSS**
TO HIS HOME & FAMILY
CONTACT CHICAGO POLICE
(312)744-8266

Missing since Nov. 21, 2006

Oct 27th, 2010

Don and Donna Ross
15706 Lawrence Ave
Belton MO 64012

Lt. D
35105 S. Michigan Avenue
Chicago, IL 60653

Lt. D,

I would ask you to look at your letter and ask yourself: If this were my son, would I take comfort in this letter? Four years and not a single new initiative on the part of the Chicago police.

Would this bring comfort to you and all your friends and family who hold Jesse near to their hearts?

When you have done all you can, you must reach deeper and do more. No single missing person should go unfound. I know you have many missing to think of, but Jesse is ours and if I could arm myself and take to the streets of Chicago, I would. But this is a civilized time, so we depend on you and yours. Apparently it is not that civilized or our son would be home.

Place this letter somewhere so your detectives can see it and ask them to go beyond the usual, to consider all possibilities. You can not know what it is like to rise each day and face the real live nightmare of a missing loved one. But that should not stop you all from burning with a desire to see our son home, or to apprehend those who have taken him from us.

Sincerely,
Don, Donna, and Andy Ross

During 2010, in August and September two men bicycled across the US,

As part of a project called *Ride for Their Lives*. The basic info on this event as taken from their Facebook page follows:

About	THE PURPOSE: Ride for Their Lives is a National Surviving Parents Coalition (SPC) Campaign seeking to raise public awareness and capital funds to assist in helping to STOP PREDATORY CRIMES against children and young adults.

The Ride For Their Lives is dedicated to preventing sexual abuse and abduction. |
| **Company Overview** | Your donations will be used to support the DNA on Felony Arrest Act, radKids, the Adam Walsh Act and the Protect Act of 2003, very important causes to the Surviving Parents Coalition. |
| **Mission** | Donations many be made online safely and easily via PayPal.

We are dedicated to conduct public awareness and prevention education campaigns to promote best practices for child protection, youth empowerment and sex offender management. |
| **Website** | http://www.ridefortheirlives.com/ |

The riders, Ed Smart and Ahmad Rivazfar two members of the Surviving *Parents Coalition*, were members of families who know first hand the horror of a kidnapped child. Their commitment to this amazing ride is another example of victims refusing to be victims and becoming a source of empowerment for others. As has happened before we were part of a smaller group, but the energy and determination was incredible.

Donna and I travelled to North Kansas City and had the honor of being among those to greet the riders as they made their way through Kansas City.

We again attended the *Project Jason* Retreat in 2010. There were many familiar faces and some new ones. We were still a family of a missing, but Donna and I found ourselves sharing our experiences and re-enforcing the coping skills that the 'newbie's' were encountering at their first retreat experience. Seeing the old familiar faces of both staff and families was comforting to say the least. Kelly arranged a candle lighting ceremony at a local chapel. The chapel sat in open country on a high rise and had a tremendous few for miles. One could sit and watch the sunset. Kelly's niece sang some wonderful songs; Christina Fontana was on hand to record the event for her documentary. To make things really interesting, the last day we awoke and Kelly had us gather in a field. There sat a hot air balloon! We all had rides, it was so amazing. Kelly had us write down the negative things we wanted to leave behind; We took them up into the air in our Balloon and threw them out. (Kelly's folk's being socially responsible gathered the papers. It was a wonderful experience.)

The Band *A Dead Giveaway*, Made up of Bryce Veazey, Jesse Collins, Jon'Bear' Gibbons, Brandon 'Woody' Woodall, and Cory Tittle approached us with the idea for a major promotion for Jesse's cause. In the summer of 2010, They planned a 10 day multi-state tour and concert, featuring Jesse and other missing, as well as local missing in each of the cities they would play in. Andy and I decided we would travel to St. Louis by air and join the band going on to Chicago and then returning to Kansas City for a final performance. The devotion and energy is amazing.

Also in September of this 2010 We joined Jim and Rhonda Beckford and other families of the missing, at a Longview lake for a Remembrance Day for Kara Kopetsky and other missing in our area. I remember it was windy, signs kept blowing down, but we all have faced more than a little wind in our quest for answers. We met couples with missing loved ones, that we were completely unaware of, right in our own area. It is easy to see why the missing can be overlooked in the hectic rush of life. All the more reason we all have to make an extra effort to be aware, and to make others aware.

We all shared good times and good food, and our 'missing' stories. We had a balloon release at the end of day; I attached a card with Jesse's info on our balloon. It was so kind of Jim and Rhonda to share this day with us.

One of our online friends sent us this message. She first requested info for her newspaper. She was also doing an online radio show and wanted to feature Jesse

Gwen J has sent you a message on Cold Case Public Unit

Subject: Donald could you please write an article for our news paper

If you could write one about your family and Jessie and how he came up missing etc. From then to now and how you guys are feeling and getting through things.

What helps you to continue to never give up. I would appreciate it you can send it to my xxxxxxxxxxxxxxxxx email and in the subject put Jessie Opie's

Story I would so love it. Let me know if you can do it and if so it will need to be done by the 24th of this month October. Thank you so much Donald just want people to know about our folks here.

I wrote the following:

Jesse Warren Ross aka Jesse 'Opie' Ross (Opie was his character name on 95.7 the Vibe radio with Shorty and the Boyz). My name is Donald Ross, Jesse's father.

Early on the morning of November 18th, 2006, Jesse woke me up about 5:00 am. His mother was asleep. We didn't see the need for both of us to get up at such an ungodly hour. He needed to be at UMKC, his school, by 6:00 am to ride to Chicago for the Model UN convention. He was traveling with 13 other students and would be there 4 days. I arrived at UMKC, and dropped Jesse in a small parking lot where one of his friends was waiting. I would have stayed around but they were talking and having so much fun, I didn't want to interfere; I drove off and waved to Jesse as I left. He kept talking to his friend and waved back as I passed. That was last time I saw my son.

On the 21st Jesse was to call around 1:00 pm and let us know he was on his way home. Instead I received a call from one of the sponsors for UMKC informing me that Jesse was missing and they were getting ready to leave. I believe I got a second call later informing me they were packing up all the other students to leave and one of the sponsors was staying to work with the police in trying to locate Jesse.

Later we learned Jesse had been staying at The Sheraton Four Points and had attended a meeting at another hotel around 1:00 A.M (a mock security council meeting). At around 02:30 a break was called and Jesse got up from his chair and exited the meeting room thru the back doors.

. That is the last time that we know of that anyone has seen him.

(It should be noted, there is a video shot of Jesse in A lobby area around some elevators. It has been printed and repeated that this video was taken when he left the meeting. Actually it is a shot of him getting ready to enter the elevator at the Sheridan Four Points where he was staying, before he went to the meeting at the conference hotel).

We had very little contact with police until later; According to police, 21 detectives searched the area; they employed cadaver dogs, boats with sonar, divers, the Coast Guard, and helicopters. Police viewed video from the hotel and neighboring business's. His cell and credit cards showed no activity. Police have no clues; they say "Jesse just vanished". We informed family and friends and they became our support network. It is impossible to describe the terrible sense of loss and fear that engulfed our lives. Initially my wife, my son Andy, and my self became a unit. We drew inward and surrounded ourselves with a wall of love. Then as time drug on We had to face the reality of our new situation and we began to reach out to family and friends that had been hovering nearby.

Now almost 4 years later, we still depend on the support of our faith, family and friends. We don't just live life we savor every person and thing that makes life worthwhile. We accept that we are not in control but we must do everything we can to get Jesse back. We must never lose hope, but we refuse to curl up and die. We will continue living as Jesse lives, energetic and with a passion for life. We do this because Jesse would have it that way. And we have survived because of the strength of those family and friends who have been there for us. We have learned we are not alone and others live with the same terrible loss. They have become members of our family as well, and together we stand, where alone we could not.

We still use the internet and mail to seek clues to Jesse's whereabouts. We work with various agencies for the missing. Each November we have 'Opiefest', an awareness/ fundraiser for Jesse. Just recently we took part in a 10 day concert tour with a band called A Dead Giveaway, featuring Jesse and other missing persons. Jesse was manager for this band for some time. I have traveled to Chicago several times, twice with the band.

We attend church regularly, it is a bitter sweet experience because our faith and church family are so supportive, yet it is a constant reminder of the way things were, and the way they are. But we have always turned to God for our strength and his love and the love of the good people around us sustains us. We will never ever ever give up.

There is a line from an old hymn:

"*If we never meet again this side of heaven, we will meet on that beautiful shore*"

That is the hope on which we have built our strength to face tomorrow.

I would like to make a note here; Someone probably will notice, that I have occasionally been a little loose with the facts. I have striven in my writing and in the information I have provided to others, to be as accurate as possible. Again I recall the words of Duane Bowers,the counselor at our retreat explaining the fatigue and confusion that often is part of our lives when we are dealing with the loss of a loved one. Often we remember things differently at different times. I apologize if I have mislead anyone, and can only promise to do my best to keep this book as factual as possible.

Below is a copy of the script I prepared for the web-broadcast show I did with Gwen J. I start to lose count of all the terrific people who reached out to us.

Jesse "Opie" Ross ; Unsolved Cases USA Script

Good Evening and welcome to Unsolved Cases USA, I am your show host Gwennie J. Tonight we will featuring the case of Jesse "Opie" Ross and will be speaking with his father Donald.

Opening Statement

On November 21st, 2006, 19 year old Jesse "Opie" Ross Disappeared. He was supposed to make a call home to his Mother Donna and to his father Donald, but in a 30 minute time frame during a break from a mock United Nations Conference that connection to home changed. Tonight we will here the story and information from his father Donald who was gracious enough to bring his story here and share it with us.

Please answer after I read these Questions or statements, they are numbered in the order I will ask them.

Welcome Donald to Unsolved Cases USA! Its a pleasure to have you with us this evening.

Now Donald before we get started into the case information itself, could you give us a background on Jesse and what type of a Person he was?

Jesse is a bighearted, outgoing young man, very brash and bold but with a soft spot in his heart for his friends and family. Very determined about what he wants to do, but willing to listen to others. He was involved in his education, in various extracurricular and civic activities and with his job.

Jesse was a sophomore student at the University of Missouri Kansas is that correct.

Yes, he was. He is a communications major and political minor. The model UN conference was part of his commitment to politics.

Donald, he was also the host of a radio show could you tell us about Jesses Work there and what that was like for him?

Jesse was an unpaid intern with 95.7 the Vibe in KC, his on air name was Opie Cunningham, taken from two of Ron Howards better known roles on *the Andy Griffith show* and *Happy Days*. He helped set up on remote locations, and was often involved in pranks and promotions with his colleagues on the morning show. Part of his initiation was to call the station manager and call him a 'big dummy' at least 5 times during the conversation. We actually have an audio recording of this event. Also Jesse once went out to an undisclosed location and callers had to listen to clues and guess where he was. I think they called it "Where's Opie?" which became the theme for one of our t-shirts. Jesse was to become a full paid employee in January, I believe, a couple of months after his return from Chicago.

Jesse was also starting a second job with a local voice over internet company and He was starting a new session of classes at UMKC. Jesse was also involved with a band called

A Dead Giveaway. Jesse had worked at a movie theatre and met one of the members of this band. He recruited the band for his senior project in high school. Jesse featured a battle of the bands in order to raise money for charity. Later he took on the role of manager for the band. Just in the last three years, I have traveled with the band on tour to spread the word about Jesse and others like him. These are a wonderful group of guys and they have become like family to us.

Do you feel Donald that there would have been anyone who may have wanted Jesse gone either from his college or his Radio Station?

There are no clues at this time that might make us think that. As a radio personality, he did interact with listeners and there may have been some negative experiences, but nothing stands out.

Now Jesse Disappeared from a Mock United Nations Conference, do you have any information regarding any suspicious activity at the conference regarding Jesse?

This was a mock emergency Security Council meeting, that is why it took place so late. Jesse left at break time, about 2:30 am, the meeting lasted until around 6:00 A.M. His roommate was at the meeting until 6. We can only suppose Jesse had something he wanted to do at this time. We were told that he might have gone back to his hotel room, 10 minutes away, to rest, having had a full day. There is no doubt in our minds that something did happen, either in the hotel or elsewhere. Police have no evidence Jesse ever left the hotel, alive.

So what time frame did Jesse Disappear in?

Jesse was last seen at about 2:30 am, leaving the meeting room. It wasn't until maybe 1:00 pm that afternoon that sponsors became concerned. No one is prepared for something like this, so a lot of time passed before anyone began to look for Jesse.

So then At about 2:30 a.m., about 12 hours after his last cell phone call to his mother, Jesse got up from his chair and walked out of the room for a 30-minute break. A surveillance camera in the hotel lobby caught the unmistakable image of the red-haired Jesse, clad in a white T-shirt, jeans, and a green warm-up jacket, walking toward the main doors. Was this the last time then Jesse was ever seen?

A number of news reports were incorrect, the surveillance footage came from the Sheraton Four Points. It was in their lobby as Jesse was going to the elevators to leave and return to the Sheraton Office and Towers for the meeting. There are no photos of Jesse after he left the meeting. There were photos of Jesse at a sponsored party with friends, I believe these were just before the meeting? Jesse's roommate stated that he saw Jesse go out the double doors at the rear of the meeting room. This is the last time anyone saw our son, that we know of.

I took an excerpt from his page that says, The 10-minute walk back to Sheraton Chicago Hotel & Towers, where Jesse and the UMKC group was staying, was well-lit, heavily traveled and covered by outdoor security cameras. None of them recorded Jesse. I want to ask you Donald was there an area at all that was not covered by camera's and If so, What was that area like?

To clarify, Jesse stayed at the Sheraton Inn at Four Points(is was more economical than the Sheraton in Office and Towers, where the meeting was held, plus with the conference in town there was a shortage of accommodations.) The area between the hotels was well light mostly, well traveled and we were told students were coming and going most of the day and night. There were a number of cameras in the area, according to police, but a review of these videos showed nothing. Again I would say police have never established that Jesse left the Office and Towers.

There was a statement Donna Made about him being Abducted by Aliens, and she said that was no more ridiculous than any other reason he might have disappeared. What does Donna feel about the possibilities of the other options, one being suicide, secondly Jesse just walking away from his life? Do you think maybe he was under to much pressure and things were stressful to him?

Donna was expressing our frustration at the lack of clues in this case. We are not prepared to accept that he just disappeared and we don't feel the police should either. Suicide never occurred to us, Jesse had too much to return to and in phone calls home he was upbeat and positive. Neither would he walk away from his school, his home, his work, his family and friends. There is no doubt in our minds that Someone is responsible for Jesse not coming home, and that it is in the hands of the Chicago police to bring those persons to justice and find our son.

This is an extremely Disturbing Case for the fact that Chicago police have found no evidence that he was a victim of foul play. There has been no activity on Jesse's credit cards or his cell phone since he disappeared into the Chicago night.

This occurred in a public place, fingerprints or DNA probably wouldn't help; You can't get a group and search the area(like a field). Police interviewed about 100 people on the scene. I guess the late hour made things difficult. The fact that sponsors waited so long to notify police and that so many who were there were already going home when police got into it. Initially Police had detectives flood the area, they searched with dogs, boats, divers, sonar, helicopters. The East river just behind the hotel has been a dumping ground for bodies dating back to the gangster days. But the river revealed nothing. A group of people and 2 former detectives, I believe from NY, had started a list of young college men who drowned or were missing and a 'happy face' symbol was found near the scene of a number of these crimes. Chicago cleans their graffiti periodically so any symbols would have been gone.

Do you have any possible leads at all since the case has been opened?

Project Jason in Ne distributed Jesse's picture and story to a network of truckers they work with. One of these persons thought he saw an individual like Jesse in Texas. In Canada some one on an internet shopping site thought they saw a picture of Jesse on that site. No real leads have materialized.

How as parents do you continue on and continue hope for Jesse?

We feed on the love and support of family and friends. Our church family has carried us when we couldn't go on alone. Agencies like Project Jason, Peace for the Missing, The National agency for missing and exploited children, Individuals from all over the world have expressed their best wishes for our son. Our faith in God has helped us realize we are not alone and that we have to be strong for all those others who are or may be in our situation. We live on the hope of being re-united with Jesse in this life or the next.

Donald are there any websites or links you would like to share with us at this time regarding Jesse? Also if you would happen to have any contact information you might want to share with them at this time.

I would like to share some information if I may: On Nov 19th, we will be hosting an awareness/fundraising event at our church, called Opiefest 5. We have done this annually since Jesse's disappearance. There will be food, music, raffle items, a guest speaker from Project Jason and hopefully another chance to put Jesse in the public eye.

Jesse is featured all over the internet, if you do a search for **Jesse Ross Missing** you will find any number of sites. During the early weeks of our ordeal, Jesse was featured in the media coast to coast. The only reason we can think of for not getting results, is that someone has intentionally done their best to prevent this from happening and we hope the police will do their best to bring Jesse back to us, or at least bring us some knowledge of what has happened to Jesse.

There are posters on some of these sites that list contact info and there is a $10,000 reward. Some better known sites are:

peace4missing.ning.com/   http://WWW.findjesseross. com www.projectjason.org/

I'd just like to say we appreciate this opportunity to present Jesse's case. At this time the effort by individuals like yourself to keep Jesse in the public eye, is one of the most important tools we have at our disposal. Thank you Gwennie.

I want to thank you Donald and Thank your lovely Wife Donna for sharing this story with us, and for offering Jesse's information to our public. I hope that we to can have another show where the outcome is much different than this one, where there is an answer or resolution to Jesse's Case. Listeners if you have any information on Jesses Case I would urge you to contact Chicago Police Department at: 312-744-8266 or you may email them at: This website http://findJesseross.com

Thank you again Donald and may you have a beautiful day.

Thank you listeners for being here to share our story and I hope you will join us again for upcoming shows on Unsolved Cases USA.

With a missing loved one, there are few things we wouldn't do. Quiet, unassuming Don and Donna on the television, on the radio; Telling and retelling Jesse's story until we are so tired. Not tired of sharing the story but just tired.

Opiefest 5 took place at St. Regis Catholic church, our parish. *The Burnt Ends*, a local church founded Bluegrass band and A Dead Giveaway were featured. Attendance was record breaking. We ran out of food, but no one complained. My brother and his wife, my nieces all came from Wichita. My son Andy, who had sworn off any Jesse related activities—he just wants Jesse back—, was there. The band *A Dead Giveaway*, performed the song they had written especially for Jesse, Opie's song:

> *Baby boy is calling from Chicago*
> *He says don't worry mama I'll be home tomorrow*
> *They're taking me places I've never seem before*
> *And I wanna see you and dad*
>
> *Then the call comes in*
> *And word spreads like fire*
> *Well I may be young but I know*
> *That none of us simply disappear*
>
> *Where are you Opie?*
> *You've been gone too long*

Where are you Opie?
I wish I'd never had to write this song

What could we know?
About being afraid
Until we see what he saw that night
It haunts my mind it haunts my mind

Where are you Opie?

You've been gone too long
Where are you Opie?
I wish I'd never had to write this song
I wish I'd never had to write this . . . .

On a sad note, Ralph Parker, Jesse's close friend, former high school and college friend, his roommate and partner at the Model UN conference where Jesse disappeared, was killed in a car accident in September of 2010. We met Ralph at *Opiefest 4*, a really sweet guy, but we didn't really get a chance to know him. Now he was gone, this part of Jesse, this link to our son, and a treasure in his own right was gone. Our hearts went out to Ralph's friends and family, many of whom we found through our association with Ralph. These were Jesse's friends also.

Media coverage for *Opiefest 5* was phenomenal. We did interviews; Reporters were there when we rolled it all up, taping and commenting on the activities. We raffled off various items. Donna and I had a cake made up for the *Dead Giveaway* guys; The band was growing and

the members were beginning to reach out in different directions. So we had the cake made with the band's picture on it. The band informed us they were pursuing different interests and would be performing individually or with other groups. They assured us we could call on them for any Jesse related activities.

The Burnt Ends Bluegrass band members were friends from church as well as accomplished musicians. We were proud that they volunteered for each Opiefest that came along. Also their music was more for us than Jesse, but I am sure if he were there he would have been happy to hear them.

Preparing for *Opiefest 5* in 2010, we sent invitations, some over the internet. One young person responded "Why are you having a party?, you should be out looking for your son?". Some said "how cruel" but upon thinking about this we realized to someone not in our position it seemed like a valid question. One of the survival tips we learned, is that you have to keep looking for your lost one, which we did. But you also have to take care of yourself. We had seen and heard of families torn apart by their loss and the different ways in which each member dealt with this loss. We were encouraged by those who had missing loved ones, much longer, to take care of ourselves. We would be no good to our loved ones unless we did. Opiefest represented a chance to raise funds, to bring awareness, (t is a must that your missing be in the public eye), and to laugh, cry, remember, share, with family, friends and other missing families. We featured posters and info(a friend had created these wonderful things called table toppers. Displays with photos and information on various missing persons). on other missing as well as Jesse. You can only cry so many tears for your loved one, then you must find time to laugh, to appreciate what you have even when you have lost. Many persons in the world are suffering terribly; Crime, natural disaster, war.

If you forget how to laugh, how to give thanks for what you <u>do </u>have, you are doomed.

Your missing or deceased love one would not want to see you suffer. Grieve as you must but, live, love, laugh.

A really special treat for us at this years Opiefest, was having Kelly Jolkowski from *Project Jason* as our featured speaker; She also brought key members of her staff. These were professional people, but also friends of ours.

Just let me say on a personal level, I had no idea just what Kelly would be sharing; I introduced her and made remarks that she would be sharing information about Project Jason. Instead she informed me that she was going to read a piece she had written. A very personal piece that shed a light into her heart and what it is like to be a parent of a missing person. I dare say, when she finished speaking, I doubt there was a person in the room that didn't have a much clearer picture of what it is like living day to day, waiting, hoping, and praying for the return of a loved one. Donna and I live that everyday, but we were still moved by the power in her narrative.

Kelly and her staff have meant so much to us, as friends and as professionals in the 'missing' business. Thank you all for enriching our lives, especially you Kelly; knowing that you carry your own burden and are still willing to lend a hand with so many others simply amazes us. We were thrilled to have friends and activists Katy Bond and Maureen Reintjes present. We often deal with faceless persons via Facebook, or email. It is such a pleasure to actually meet these wonderful people face to face.

In December of 2010, we had been contacted by a producer from Lifetime TV. She had formerly been with John Walsh's *America's Most Wanted*. She informed us that she had been thinking about our story for some time. It had not really been the type of story *AMW* was looking for, but in her new position working for Lifetime, she became aware of a new series about the missing, called *Vanished*. Hosting this new series would be Beth Holloway, mother of Natalee Holloway, the young woman who disappeared in Aruba in 2005 and made national headlines. Beth has made national headlines in her relentless quest to find Natalee, and bring those responsible for her disappearance, to justice. We spent time in and around our home with a wonderful crew, taping and talking about Jesse. Much like my experiences in Chicago with the media,

A handful of specialists showed up at our house. A camera person, a sound person, A director/producer. The house became a makeshift recording studio. They took shots around Belton and even followed me to Jesse's school. We were treated well; all of these people were professionals and treated us very well. Donna, Andy and I became part of the whirlwind of activity that takes place in creating the quality of story the Lifetime people were looking for, and at the same time we were treated as human beings, not extras in some Hollywood production.

CHAPTER 6

2011

Later in January of 2011, after the flurry of the first tapings for Lifetime had died down, We received a phone call. Lifetime wanted to know if they could fly us to San Diego to meet Beth, and to tape some further sequences. Donna gave me one of her 'what have you gotten us into' looks, but soon was caught up in the excitement.

I would like to pause here to allow an insight into the world of a family of a missing. Donna once told me this was all like being pregnant. Your hormones are all out of sort, you spend most of your time trying to decide whether to laugh or cry. San Diego! television! It was all very exciting, but a cloud hovered over this experience as it did over all others. When the noise dies down, you are left with this hollow feeling in your chest.

Where's Opie? We are doing all these things, have been for over 4 years, but it just seems we are putting on a show. The police are silent; no clues come in. And we miss our son. We want to hold him, to say how much we love him, to hear him laugh and crash up and down the basement stairs again. No amount of hoopla or grand standing can replace the reality that he is gone. Where's Opie?

We have followed Beth's story and we saw her become a force for the missing and families of the missing. And with our unique perspective, we also saw the hollow feeling she carried, that could never be filled until her lost one is brought home, one way or another.

Back on track, Donna and I agreed to go to San Diego; We arrived there in January of 2011. We made arrangements to take Andy with us, He was involved in the taping, and actually did an interview with the crew in Belton. It is hard to say what goes through the mind of another, even your own son. We sat and listened to Andy talk about Jesse and heard for the first time some of the feelings he was carrying around inside. Andy has always told us he would do anything if it would get Jesse back, but he did not want to do the television, newspapers, all the circus like activities. Donna and I both understood this feeling. Andy was not part of the original deal with Lifetime to go to San Diego, but we made our own arrangements for him to be there.

San Diego was wonderful. It took time for all the crew, staff members etc to get organized, so we were able to see some of the city. Again part of us was in vacation mode, part in the working for Jesse mode. It is difficult to explain the torrent of feelings that seem to constantly tear at us. This is probably what Andy did not want to deal with. We had a very interesting time with the taping. Sat down for an in-depth interview with Beth, surrounded by crew members.

Everyone had some portion of the proceedings to deal with and we would often stop for some kind of 'fix' and then we would roll on. A professional make-up artist worked on Donna and I. Donna was quite glamorous

The lady was a great makeup artist, not great enough to make me look like Chuck Norris (as I suggested), but great none-the-less.

While in San Diego we had the pleasure of dining with friends, Maureen Barton and her husband JB. Their son Brian Barton disappeared in March of 2005. http://www.amw.com/missing_persons/case.cfm?id=56390

May 9th, 2011 We travelled to Michigan. It was our desire to see Lake Michigan, and Grand Haven. Grand Haven is the home of our dear friend Sara, of *Peace4 the Missing*. This was to be a getaway for Donna and I, we had not had a vacation on this scale in years. We wanted to stay lakeside, see some lighthouses, and spend some quality time with Sara and family. Steve and Sara were so great; We had dinner with them twice; they filled us in on the local sites. And the local citizens were so warm and friendly; we got a first hand view of the community gearing up for the summer crowds. It was really rather quiet when we were there, which we liked. I could just imagine the excitement and the crowds for the summer; Maybe next year.

We also planned for two Jesse related events: 1) to stop in Chicago on the way home, and 2)to attempt to see M, a new friend who was actually with Jesse much of the time he was in Chicago. M lived just about two hours from Grand Haven. M came to our attention during our time with the *Lifetime* people. Their researchers located M and interviewed her. We had actually seen her in pictures of Jesse in Chicago, but we had no clue of her identity. In her interview with *Lifetime* producers, new information was discovered. M contacted us when Lifetime requested to interview with her. We gave our permission and in an extended call, she talked with me about what she knew. Apparently after Jesse disappeared, M and the other students were approached by a sponsor and told not to talk to us about Jesse's time in Chicago. They were told we were grieving. This was interesting because we had been talking with the sponsors at that time, expressing our interest in speaking with the people who saw our son last. We had four days of Jesse's life that we had no part in and we just wanted to hear from those fortunate enough to be with him. The sponsors agreed that they would speak to the students and try to arrange something. Each time we made this request they returned saying the students did not want to meet with us. M also shared her concern that one of the sponsors could have negative influence on her academics if she did not cooperate. So sponsors were telling us that students did not want to meet, and students were told to stay away from us. This around the time the school was telling us "Anything you need let us know". Apparently when Lifetime contacted M she realized she needed to talk to us. She likewise shared with us that the police had minimal contact with her. They did not ask about any of the information she shared with us; They simply asked 3 questions, thanked her and hung up. She felt they had already made up their minds about what happened. Again M shared additional information. She had gone with Jesse to a bar, apparently because he had some music and was interested in making some Chicago contacts to help promote his cds. We had heard about these cds from others but nothing came of it. She also said he planned on visiting a local radio station again to promote his music. M further assured us that she saw a bright yellow flyer advertising a rave. We had heard of this flyer and that one was actually in Jesse's room. Of course by the time police got there, the room was cleaned out, all this type of material thrown away.

Police had told us early on, that they did no investigations beyond the hotel, they felt they had no reason to do so because they had found no evidence Jesse went anywhere'; they believed with the parties and so on, Jesse would have had no reason to leave the hotel. They discounted the idea of the cds, no cds were ever found. They also said they never saw any flyers and would have no idea where to start investigating this rave. Everyone did everything wrong, even Donna and I, we were all unprepared for this kind of thing; when they brought Jesse's things home we just packed them away. But the actual withholding of information, as well as denying us access to those students that were in attendance, this was a more deliberate attempt to cover up facts, despite the potentially negative impact on the police investigation. Looking at the way police haphazardly contacted M, we began to wonder just how they had conducted the other interviews they told us that they had conducted. We were told that they called the school, and asked campus police to do interviews here in Kansas City. Police never came to our home or interviewed us, or looked for evidence here in Belton. I will repeat, the initial physical search for clues in Chicago, looking for Jesse's body, was thorough by all accounts; But some of the areas of investigation; interviewing witness, discovering key information about Jesse's movements, these issues were handled in a very questionable manner.

And the possibility of misconduct on the part of school officials and their representatives, nagged at us. The sponsor in question, D, also interviewed with Lifetime. We obtained copies of these transcripts. D's testimony read more like a defense of what he did and didn't do. He seemed more interested in building himself up and seemed not to realize

Jesse was the reason for this investigation. Maybe I have read something into all this, but that was my impression.

Jesse's story is due to air on June 20th, 2011. We will see what this brings out, then we will have to decide if there is some action we can take that will benefit Jesse's case. Because that is what this is all about; finding Jesse, one way or another, and bringing justice to him and those who may be responsible for his disappearance.

We have never heard the police revise their opinion that they did not suspect foul play. We know better; Our son would be home if he could be. We believe police embrace the theory that he walked away, simply because that is the theory that reflects best on them.

Note: The detective on our case when asked about the 'Lifetime' show, remarked "I haven't see it."

Meanwhile, certain events did not come about.

Firstly M was in Missouri, the state we just left on personal business. Secondly, well the fact is we enjoyed Grand Haven so much we stayed an extra day. We just didn't have it in us to take on the challenge of the huge busy metropolis of Chicago and the apathy of police.

Fact is, we felt good and didn't want to let go of those positive feelings. Were we being selfish? Maybe we were. We had no real game plan for Chicago. Our plans to meet our PI there fell through. Also we had plans to be back in Illinois somewhere for June 18th—Missing and Unidentified Persons Day in Illinois. So we started the long trip home

Much as we adored Grand Haven and our time there, it was good to get home.

Someone had suggested we should petition the office of Pat Quinn, Governor of Illinois to proclaim June 18th, 2011 as Missing and Unidentified Person's Day in Illinois. Using guidelines provided by supporters we put together a petition. We sent it to the Gov.s office. Friends in Chicago promised to help with our efforts.

We received in the mail, a large envelope. It was from the Governor's office! Inside was a beautiful document proclaiming June 18th as Missing and Unidentified Person's Day in Illinois. Mission accomplished. But wait! Someone said "go to Chicago on the 18th and take your proclamation". There was that 'what have you gotten me into' look in Donna's eye again. This time it was what have we gotten ourselves into.

So this launched two events through Facebook. Firstly, a virtual event asked people all over to support and recognize this day. Secondly, an actual onsite event in Chicago was planned, at which we would be present with friends and other families of the missing.

We communicated with the Gov.s office about his participation. A very nice scheduler took our information. She said she would get back. Still waiting as of June 6th. (Never received a reply)

Actually we weren't just waiting. We called city officials at another suggested site, Normal Illinois. Normal is much closer to us than Chicago, and has a number of beautiful parks, available for use at no charge. We selected a shelter near the water park, a very high profile area. We then issued invitations to families of the missing thru *Facebook* and some contacts we had with Missing Person's activists in Chicago. Being our first such event we were putting things together as we went and would probably be surprised to see the final result. We created an online committee made up of many of our old and new friends in the 'missing' field.

The helpful lady from Normal had advised me that the shelter was designed for up to 200 people. I didn't want that many since we had displays to set up, and didn't know just what kind of real space we would need. Still I wasn't really worried. That is until I looked at the 'event' page on Facebook. Some very helpful person had gotten a little over-enthusiastic and we had 600 people listed in the 'invited' field! I could see the tree and the rope that the Normal folks would use to hang me if their park was mobbed by 100's of 'missing' enthusiasts.

To date(June 6, 2011) There are 31 confirmed attendees. As I said this was our first event and a work in progress. We sent notices to the Governor, The Mayor of Chicago, and Chicago police. So far the only officials we have heard from came through our Chicago friends for the missing who made contacts through their personal acquaintances.

On June 16th, we received an email from the office of Representative Dan Brady. According to the email, He had just become aware of our event and was going to try to make an appearance. This is the first response we had from a government official since the Governor responded with the proclamation. We actually have to thank Cinda L with Illinois State Patrol for contacting Rep. Brady.

When I was in scouting with my sons, There was a standing joke; Become a scout leader, only one hour a week. Anyone with scouting experience knew that the one hour a week was actual meeting time; There was no mention of the hours upon hours of camping, preparation for camping, meetings, and other events. As well as time spent working with parents of scouts.

This is the feeling you get when working for a cause; whether it be a missing, the abused, domestic violence, or any number of causes. One hour a week expands into doing whatever it takes. No time clock. "The harder I work the behinder I get", some sage put it. We started with just a simple little event for the missing and then found ourselves drowning in details.

During the planning of this event, there were several misunderstandings and tempers did flare a bit; But when putting together any enterprise that involves so many different parties, we have to realize everyone is contributing in someway We don't always agree or communicate(long distance no less), but we get things done.

Update on Normal event, now it seems there are 15 attendees. Oh well, don't worry be happy.

Monday June 13th. I awoke at 10:00. I missed my 9:30 appointment, not to sleep to 10. Since I got my weight bench I have been working out three days a week. Feels good during the day, but I still wake up with my shoulders feeling like I have been toting water all night. Only one real cure for old, and I'm not ready for that yet. Sitting in the kitchen typing away, Donna has already been at the other pc maybe an hour, working on documents and displays for Saturday. A million questions for me since I am the computer support in this house. "How do I get this over there? Can I copy this and put it in that?" I am glad to help but I haven't had my Corn Fruities and milk yet.

Tuesday, June 14th 2011, Met with Michael Tabman, Former FBI agent, author, and Security Consultant. Michael shared some insights on writing, which I greatly appreciated. We met Michael and co. thru a mutual friend. He took a very personal interest in Jesse's story, and was able to give us advice and to work with some contacts to clarify certain issues we had with law enforcement. Michael is a late-comer to Jesse's case, but we continue to look to him for personal and professional guidance. Michael and his lovely wife were guests at our Opiefest V event. Their simple presence gave us a warm sense of well-being. To learn more about Michael visit this website http://michaeltabman.com/

Spoke with a person from the *Missing Person's Clearinghouse for Illinois State Police*. She was trying to be really helpful, but I think it is difficult for some to realize what it is like to be a family with a missing member. We talked on the phone and established groundwork for future communications. Sorry but I talk like that when I talk to Govt. people; no sarcasm intended, hopefully we may have a new contact for getting things done in Illinois. Most of us who have had a missing for some time are often skeptical of offers of help, until we see results. It does, however, pay to keep an open mind.

Donna is working on posters and displays for **Missing and Unidentified Person's Day in Illinois** on Saturday. It occurs to me that we are not doing this event because we are good at events, we are doing this because there is a need.

I suddenly feel the need for some comic relief, so here goes.

Bob from the city is invited to go fishing with Bo from the country.

They arrive at the lake and go out in Bo's boat. Bo stops at a likely place, pulls out a stick of dynamite, lights it, and drops it in the water. "Boom". Dead fish float to the surface everywhere.

"Isn't that illegal?" Bob asks.

Bo turns, looks at him, and replies "You come to talk or fish?"

Now if you are named Bob or Bo and you are sitting in a boat 'fishing', I must advise that all persons mentioned in this joke are, to the best of my knowledge, fictitious.

Vanished With Beth Holloway Episode: "Kopetsky; Ross"

Season 1, Episode 6

Episode Synopsis: A teen's disappearance is preceded by the filing of her missing-person report; a boy vanishes while on a school trip to Chicago. **Original Air Date: Jun 20, 2011—Listing from television guide website.**

June 20th, a Monday, is just around the corner. Jesse and a young lady, Kara Kopetsky, who disappeared right here in our home town, Belton MO, will be featured on Lifetime television. In a previous chapter I talked about our adventure with the Lifetime people; well this is the culmination of all that activity. On the 20th we will see what the viewing public sees. What will come of all of this? We can't say, but short of going out and bringing Jesse home(oh that we could), this is the best we can do. There is always the hope that someone will see this and feel something for us, or for Kara's parents. Perhaps they will call in and give the information that brings one or both of our children home. Hope is all we have and Lifetime gives us hope. Certainly they are a business, they produce a product and need to make a profit. But above this, *Vanished* offers the opportunity to share the story of our missing loved ones. Perhaps this will appeal to legislators or police and bring about change that may not directly help us, but will be beneficial to others who find themselves where we are

We can only hope. But we do want to take this opportunity to again thank Beth and all those who made this possible.

June 17th, 2011, We came up to highway 36 and across northern Missouri into Illinois. Highway 36 runs through Hannibal, light traffic, beautiful scenery. Mark Twain territory. We encountered storms early on but it was dry and overcast most of the trip. We arrived in Normal IL, checked in at the motel. Price is right but place is so so. We went to Weaver rental and picked up a helium tank for balloons. Then we went over to the park; A very nice park; shelter right next to the park; Tennis courts, baseball fields, basketball courts, and it is a stones throw away from Illinois State University. The whole area screams "fun". Everything is good, other than Donna thinks the helium might blow us up in our car. I told her this isn't the Hindenburg.(Helium vs. hydrogen). Tomorrow is the day.

June 18th, 2011 **Missing and Unidentified Person's Awareness day**; When we arrived at the park, Grace F, Founder of **Missing Loved Ones of Illinois**, was waiting for us. She helped us set up posters and other displays within the shelter. The weather was iffy, not raining but cloudy. Also on the scene, Officer Todd Weir from the Normal traffic division. Officer Weir made himself available for any type of presentation we might wish. He agreed to be available when we contacted him. He was in the process of patrolling the area we were in. Since there were only three of us present and the pool hadn't opened yet, we felt we would wait for Officer Weir to take part. We had some people stop by and ask questions.

As the day passed we began to suspect the three of us were going to be the group. We started with 31 or so who signed up for the event. Then just before we left Belton, the number was down to 15. Maybe they thought they were signing up for the virtual event, which was to take place around the state, online. We also received a notice from the office of State Representative Dan Brady. He had been contacted by Cinda Lubich from the *Missing Person's Clearinghouse for Illinois State Police*, and invited to our gathering.

The sun came out; A few locals began to show up. I took many pictures and video. I placed posters and postcards in the office for the swimming pool. I went into the park and hung posters on everything from telephone poles, to bathroom doors.

Representative Brady walked up to the shelter and introduced himself. He seemed to be completely at ease with our small numbers. He was impressed with our displays and facts and figures. He took notes! We talked and posed for pictures with Representative Brady; we taped a segment for the internet in which the Rep. Brady commented on the day, the proclamation from the Governor, and shared with us about his work on legislation for the missing in Illinois. He called a local radio station and organized an impromptu interview between myself and Jim Fitzpatrick of WJBC radio. Jim Fitzpatrick was professional and sympathetic, his questions and comments to the point. Our time with him and Rep. Brady gave so much meaning to our event.

Later Officer Weir returned and we taped a segment for the internet in which he shared information about the Normal police, and dealing with the missing. He was exceptionally friendly, helpful and polite. We are extremely grateful to the Normal Police Department for lending their support.

As it turned out, the three of us were the group. No more attendees showed. The sky began to cloud and we packed up around 12:30 and left. Rep. Brady assured us he would speak with the Governor about participation in future events. Donna and I decided we would be part of such events but we would not take responsibility for organizing. This should be done by residents of Illinois. Perhaps with the cooperation of various members of the state government, those individuals in Illinois with missing members, may find the resources they need to bring awareness to the cause of Illinois missing and unidentified.

Donna and I returned to the motel. We ordered Chicago pizza and settled in. We went to bed early. I slept deeply

At break of day, I was dreaming. This often happens when we travel for Jesse related events. I dreamed of the boys, of the time when I would sit with them and help them with their spelling words for school. Before the time they started helping me with mine. And then I dreamt further, I must have been sleeping lighter, as I became aware of the reality of Jesse's disappearance. A feeling of sorrow and grief took hold of me; I felt a great need for comfort. At this time I seemed to sense a hand, taking hold of mine; And the warmth of another lying down next to me. I want to believe that this was Jesse reaching out to me. Who can say, maybe I just wanted this to be, but I prefer to believe he was there for me.

We left that morning for home. The previous day we had a call from our neighbors back in Belton A storm had passed through. There had been a power outage of about 12 hours There was also some damage to trees, but our trees were small so we didn't worry. Later around Hannibal MO, We checked in again and found the power had come back around midnight. Most of our return trip was sunny. When we pulled into the driveway we were happy to be home and to have power. The temperature was 90+ degrees.

June 20, 2011, D-Day, the *Vanished* episode with Beth Holloway and featuring Jesse and Kara Kopetsky, would be on at 9:00 pm. Larry and Loretta our neighbors, came over to watch *Vanished* with us. Larry is a former Marine, retired and a Vietnam veteran. I sense that he understands what it is to have life give you a kick or two. He is very understanding and seems to have endless patience with everyone. They have two grandchildren and Larry keeps them in line with a sort of gruff love. Loretta is the Sgt. Major I think. A very nice lady, but she seems to be quietly running the household like a well-oiled machine. In truth it is a partnership; they have been a couple longer than Donna and I, so things run pretty smoothly, with an occasional grinding of the gears I think. They did n ot know Jesse very well, but they had seen him coming and going.

I think back to all the taping and work the *Lifetime* crew did, and there was much of it that was not used. But the finished product was excellent. They did an amazing job of weaving all the threads into a tapestry that draws the eye of the viewer. We watched Kara Kopetsky's segment first. It too was well done; We were fascinated despite our previous knowledge of the case. In point of fact we did learn some interesting facts that we had not previously been aware of. On *Facebook*, we had invited the Beckford's, Kara's mother and stepfather, to join us; we got no reply, but sometimes they may not check their messages everyday. Plus this is a very emotional time and some of us may crave company, some may not. Certainly we will gather soon at our favorite restaurant, *Mi Pueblito*, where we have met in the past.

Jesse came to life on the screen. They traced his steps from Belton to Chicago. They showed scenes of his childhood, a happy smiling boy. A moving scene shows Jesse from some of my home video, slowly turning to face the camera. The look on his face tore at my heartstrings. Also there was a voice recording from 95.7 the vibe, in which an enthusiastic fan wants to know if 'Opie' is married. He responds "How do you feel about a guy who lives in his parent's basement?"

In reality he had a room upstairs across from ours; he also laid claim to the unfinished basement. He had a vision of a room of his own down there, a room nearly as big as the entire upstairs. Shortly before he left for Chicago, we had a bedroom built in the basement for Jesse. It was not the sprawling complex he envisioned, but it was nice. When Donna talked to him in Chicago, she let him know we had the paint for the walls. Jesse was really excited; he had plans to paint the room University of Kansas colors; this was his favorite basketball team. He also wanted to have a wall painted white so all his friends could autograph it.

We saw on screen for the first time the new detective assigned to Jesse's case. This was a man I needed to travel to Chicago to meet. I wanted to see if he had something to offer besides the sympathetic 'can't help ya son' look that we had begun to associate with Chicago law enforcement.

The show posed several theories about what happened to Jesse. They offered interviews with a number of people. The off-screen voice said "Police still think he is in the river" I seriously doubt that. With the sonar and divers and the history of finding bodies in that river, the police had assured us if he was in there he would surface in time. D the sponsor accompanying Jesse on his trip stated that "We knew nothing except that Jesse left that hotel." The reality is we don't even know that. Police have never been able to establish that Jesse ever actually left the hotel. We have so little information, for all we know Jesse could have returned to one of the party rooms; something could have gone wrong, he could have been smuggled out of the hotel.

M, a young woman who was with Jesse much of his time in Chicago, shed new light on what we knew of Jesse's time up there. We had heard stories of a music cd Jesse was wanting to promote and that he had been interested in a Rave party, where he could hook up with Chicago DJ, hopefully for career opportunities. There had been mention of a flyer for this Rave, a flyer that may have been in Jesse's room. M verified she saw this flyer, that Jesse had one. She also spoke of a bar and a radio station that Jesse had visited or intended to visit. Again we were reminded of the phone conversation we had with this young lady, in which she expressed her concern that police did not thoroughly interview those involved with Jesse's case, including her, at the time he disappeared. She likewise stated that the sponsor D and Jesse's school specifically forbade them to talk to us, when we were pleading with the sponsors to set up a meeting with students and they told us the students would not agree.

We have felt and still feel the police need to talk with D and the school concerning their actions and the possible detrimental effects on the investigation. Bad enough over 12 hours passed before any serious action was taken after Jesse disappeared. Suppose we could have gotten information to give to the police? Such a mess and we were denied the opportunity to bring some clarity.

As for the Rave, that flyer was probably thrown out when they cleaned Jesse's hotel room. As were many things, since police were not called in until Sponsors first took care of there housekeeping chores. Apparently getting the 12 remaining UMKC students out and going home took priority over our son. We understand this situation was difficult and who can say if we would have done any better. But the possibility of a deliberate cover-up of information to avoid liability on the part of the school and officials is difficult for us to comprehend. A young man was missing and someone chose to play games?

Getting back on topic, the show gave us hope; National coverage of Jesse's story; A chance for people to see Jesse as a real living human being. It is our hope, that police will go back and re-examine the case and will conduct thorough interviews with all concerned. They might say to us that nearly five years have passed; but it is not our fault they did not pursue the interview process when they had the chance. And no one has to remind us it's been nearly 5 years, we are reminded every single day.

June 22nd, we sent this email to the Billy Goat Tavern in Chicago:

> Our son Jesse Ross disappeared in Nov 2006, on the 21st. Just now we are learning he spent time in your bar. I realize not much hope but if anyone remembers anything please call at xxxxxxxxxxxx Thank you Don Ross. Jesse's story will be on *Vanished* with Beth Holloway on Lifetime television at 9:00 pm central time. (pictures attached.)

This is the bar where Jesse and M spent time. We just received this information when the Lifetime television people did their interviews. So nearly 5 years later we get information and we are asking these people for help. It is easy to see what happens when everything is not done as should be at the time of the crime. (And I do mean crime maybe more than one).

My thought for today: *Eight days a week*, a song for
   those who miss someone.
Sunday: Worship day
Monday: Start of another week of hope
Tuesday:. Kind of a useless day a that keeps Monday
   from bumping into Wednesday
Wednesday: Hump day
Thursday: Tuesday again
Friday: Cheesy old horror movie night
Saturday: Fun day(such as it is)
Wats2day: A day older persons and family members of
   the missing know all too well.

June 23rd I had a little dream of Jesse. I was trying to
get someone to help me look for him. And there he was,
as a small boy standing next to me, asking "Who's Jesse?"
Perhaps this was an expression of my frustration with the
system, a frustration shared by many.

The *Vanished* episode raised lots of questions. Made me
think about possible scenarios

1. Something happened in the hotel, at a party perhaps
   and they Smuggled Jesse out.
2. He was walking back to the hotel and was stopped by
   police. He got a little out of control and was killed.
   Police are sitting on the investigation to cover for their
   own.
3. Aliens
4. Went to the Rave and fell prey to gangs, organized
   crime of some sort.
5. Went to the Billy Goat Tavern and fell prey to
   predators.
6. Smiley Face killers?

7.   He is a drug lord living it up in the middle east somewhere.
8.   Victim of Human trafficking

You see what we are left with when we wait on the police for nearly 5 years, hoping they will come up with something. Maybe we need a contest, asking people to present their ideas. Then we can have the police pick one and pursue it. Doing nothing is not an option.

We will be going to Seymour, MO this weekend to meet with my father's family. Anymore there is a new generation; We know few of those who are there. The people we knew growing up have passed on. So we share Jesse's story with people who have never heard of us, let alone Jesse. The world keeps turning even if it stands still for us.

June 24th We are in Springfield. Tomorrow we gather with relatives, some having no clue who we are; Should be interesting.

I am inspired today, God likes to put words in my head sometimes.

I have found it is not enough to want to be a good person.
We must commit to do good in a world that often does not appreciate our efforts.
And we must do good not because we expect some reward, but because it is the right thing to do.

These words are from my facebook status. To some they may sound trite, but this is the philosophy that helps sustain us. Yes we are dealing with a family tragedy; but we are no different than anyone else, even if we see ourselves as good people. We are still subject to the same fickle whims of the world as much as anyone else. "It rains on the just and the unjust." And in point of fact if we were to read the newspapers, we would find many who are so much worse off than we are.

La Desiderata of Happiness (excerpt)
. . . . With all its sham, drudgery, and broken dreams, it is still a beautiful world.
Be cheerful.
Strive to be happy.
1927 prose poem by American writer Max Ehrmann (1872-1945)

The words above are not mine. I wish they were. But I thought of these words today and of the simple but important message they share. You can not speak these words, but you must actually live them, if they are to have validity. Note the statement

"Nurture strength of spirit to shield you in sudden misfortune."

If like us, some unforeseen event has dropped like a boulder into the middle of your life, then you need to understand and take these words to your heart. For my family and I the strength that we already possessed from our spiritual life and the relationship with supportive people, helped us to cope. How do we get this strength of spirit? We must associate with loving supportive people and we must immerse ourselves in a positive, life-affirming belief,. For us it is the Catholic faith; But for others it may be some other faith. The important thing to remember, is it must be a faith you can apply in your daily life. You cannot talk the talk, you must walk the walk. This is how I explained it to the media; We talked the talk for many years. Losing Jesse required us to walk the walk.

Donna was pregnant before Andy, our oldest, came along. Throughout her pregnancy she spoke as was the trend at the time. "We are pregnant." I was supportive but I had never been married before, let alone a parent and I wasn't sure how to feel as a prospective parent. But when Donna lost the baby suddenly the reality of the life that had been growing within her—within "us" as far as the commitment of both of us was concerned—, I felt the weight of loss come crashing down upon me. We cried together; Never before had I felt such a terrible sense of something precious taken away.

We could have gotten bitter, but Donna felt that possibly there was something wrong so God took care of the baby. But we accepted that this was the way things were meant to be. We went by our church and we made a donation in the name of our unborn child. This was our way of saying "we don't understand, but we accept".

I am not sharing this to say that we are saints; I simply want to illustrate that life does not promise a free ride because we try to be 'good' people. I have to say in all honesty, Donna's faith has been my strength. I looked at her and found the strength to live up to the words we spoke. Then when Jesse disappeared, yes we were knocked off our feet. But we were able to reach up and take hold of our faith and pull ourselves up. We could not have done this without the commitment of ourselves and others. God certainly helped us. Some look about and say "Where's God?, I don't' see him." If you have surrounded yourself with loving supporting people, no matter what their faith, you will see God; In their eyes, in their hands; In all the things they do for you, without asking or expecting thanks or reward. If you look around and those people are not there, seek them out. I told my sons, stay close to your church family, that way where ever you go you should have "family".

I guess at this point I should sit down and pass the plate. But I do think there is merit in these thoughts I have shared. Take some time and meditate on them.

June 25th We followed detours until we found ourselves late and on highway 60 headed East to Seymour. This is the location for the Ross/Yarger reunion. This was actually only a small part of our trip. We spent about two hours visiting with distant relatives, and we actually sat down with my two brothers and my sister-in-law. They live in Wichita, we live in Belton MO and we have to go all the way to Springfield MO just to see each other for a couple of hours. That's family life.

Donna and I left Seymour and returned to Ozark. We went into Springfield to our favorite combination Antique store/ flea market, where I saw a book by Sharon Sala. The following is the dedication from that book:

The older I get, the more I have begun to understand the words of my elders.

When my grandfather died, my grandmother was devastated. I remember hearing her say in a tiny, broken voice, "I thought I would go first. I didn't want to be left behind."

When my father, then my sister, died within two months of each other, our whole family was broken. Grocery lists they'd written the week before were still there, but they were not. I remember my mother's words. "No parent should outlive their child."

Long before my fiancé, Bobby ever began to get sick, he told me out of the blue one day, "If anything ever happens to me, you will be all right."

Then, when he died, I wailed in a lost, hopeless cry. "I wish I could go with him."

In the ensuing weeks after his death, I remembered his prophetic words and I was certain that he was wrong.

I know he laughs now, because time has proved that he was right.

Despite the tragedies and sorrows life hands us, there is always one undeniable truth.

As long as we draw breath, we owe it to the ones we loved and lost to live out our lives without wasting them on regrets.

So . . . just to set the record straight, you were right, my love, In honor of those we've loved and lost, I am dedicating this book to the ones who get left behind."

(Used with permission of the author)

This woman has read my mind, and touched my soul, she knows just what I am feeling. Good advice to take to heart. I have thought about death. I don't want to go and leave Donna with the burden of Jesse's disappearance; but I don't want to be left behind either. And there is Andy to think of, I don't want us both to go and leave him alone. So I have done as I try always try to do. I turn to God and say "Not my will but thine,." I'm off the hook.

I'm not suggesting you lay down and let the world roll over you, but there are times when we need to realize we don't have any control over what is happening. That is the time to de-stress and go with the flow.

I remember coming home from work one day and I was in my car, waiting to turn onto the street into my neighborhood. I looked in my rearview mirror and saw a pickup truck bearing down on me from behind. I thought he would stop. I looked again and saw he was almost on top of me, so I took a deep breath and just let myself relax all over. The impact of his vehicle pushed the trunk of my car into the back seat. When it was over it took two tow trucks and a man jumping on the bumper of my car to get us apart. But I was not even sore. If I had tensed up just at the time of impact, no doubt my neck and shoulders would have been stiff and sore; I might have even had injuries. There is a time for action and a time for just letting things go. Also I said a prayer of thanks to God for the fact that my boys were not in the backseat at the time. Yes the loss of my car(it was totaled) was bad but the loss of life would have been far worse. I stayed calm. The high school student who hit me couldn't believe I wasn't jumping up and down and screaming. It wouldn't have changed anything. This is a gift my father passed on to me. So when Jesse went missing, this lesson helped me to survive; not to say I wasn't impacted by this terrible event, but I survived.

June 27th, 2011, Speaking of survival, I am 63 today. I hope with all my heart that I live to know what has happened to our Jesse. Of course I am not in control of such things, but hope is something we all can have. I try to have goodwill towards everybody, especially family as they are the ones who can drive you buggy quickest. My family has always been prone to be wrapped up in their own lives; Donna loves them and I guess I do too. It just get frustrated doing all the reaching out. It seems like this is a fairly common phenomenon. And they don't seem to think about Jesse so much anymore. Again I guess I can't expect others to live up to my standards. After all they are <u>my</u> standards. In some ways it is like the people we have met because of Jesse, have become a new family. Not to replace the old, but to augment it. Bible says "Harden not your heart" I think I know what that means. Jesse would not want that. He expects more.

Here is a little faith exercise, think of someone who annoys you; you can hardly stand to be around them. Now think of a way to do something nice for this person. Just because it's the right thing to do. You could say a prayer for me and mine., If someone is caught for harming Jesse, perhaps causing his death, we will need prayers and all the help we can get to keep from hardening our hearts.

I once wrote '*Trouble often starts with the meeting of two hearts*. I also believe sometimes the best things in life come from the meeting of two hearts, or more. Do not underestimate the healing power of the heart; of many hearts joined in the same cause. This has become a reality for us.

I never had the chance to have the 'you're 21' speech with Jesse; to share a margarita or a glass of wine; To talk about drinking and conducting oneself responsibly. So if you have a someone getting ready to go out in the world, whatever age, tell them about Jesse. Let them know you must pursue your dreams, but not everyone who says friend is a friend. Teach them to respect themselves and to expect others to do the same. And if you can, give them a GPS phone, a small one they can hide in their shoe or where ever, so some potential predator may not find it before it can be traced. I know that sounds paranoid and rather silly, but trust me, there are very few things too trivial to do to protect our loved ones from those who don't love them.

Note: Filled out our registration for the Project Jason retreat in August. Kelly J always prepares a wonderful experience for those who need healing. It's really exciting knowing we have this to look forward to in August. There are times when looking forward is the only remedy for looking backwards.

June 28th, 2011 I do not hate animals, do not want to see them hurt; Still I am disturbed when I see primetime ads for the *ASPCA* with rich musical scores, and celebrity backers. Then I see only one show '*Vanished*' telling the story of 3 young boys, grabbed off the street; .and forced into lives of sexual slavery. Wonder how many are willing to come to the aid of those victims. The announcer tells us they would now be 40 some years old. The truth is way before 40, they outlived their usefulness and new children had to be procured. We must take care of our animals, but children come first. And this story is only one of many; Human trafficking is an epidemic that most aren't even aware of. It is difficult to believe that human beings could do such a terrible thing, but human trafficking is a huge business. So if you are a corporate sponsor or have a few thousand lying around, or a celebrity looking for a cause, join the cause. Tomorrow it could be your child.

Jessie Foster, A young Canadian woman, went missing March 29th, 2006 from Las Vegas. Her mother believes the man who became her companion is involved in human trafficking and is responsible for her disappearance. I have watched *Vanished* with Beth Holloway since its inception and I have seen episodes in which young women who disappeared were seen on numerous occasions trying to escape from traffickers. I think we all need to admit to ourselves, ignoring the existence of something because it is so evil, does not make it go away. We need to use every tool we have to stop this epidemic.

And a show like *Vanished* is not just entertainment, it is one tool for reaching out to unaware members of the public, apathetic public officials; anyone that needs to know that slavery is not dead and there is no real limit to the depths of human cruelty.

I was watching television and one of the characters says something like: "We make spaces in our lives and fill them with memories."

I can tell you, I do. If you took a tour of our house, you would find pieces of the past everywhere. Jesse gave me a book for Christmas; A Star Wars figure on another occasion; a small metal replica of '*The General*' (the car used in the *Duke's of Hazard* television series) still another time. We have gotten rid of some things that belonged to Jesse; Things we think he won't want or need <u>when </u>he comes home. The house is still full of his things. I have a small wooden box, filled with mementoes. I also have a heart full of memories that I couldn't lose if I tried. They are a part of me. I may be come old(er) and senile; That does not mean I have lost the memories, but rather I am lost in the memories. My Grandmother once sat in a chair in my Aunt Goldie's home and asked "Where is this bus going?"

That is why I urge people to go forward making good memories. That could well be where you spend your last days. Perhaps our eternal lives are shaped by the memories we make (God have mercy on those who live lives of evil and create sorrow where ever they go). The best part of making good memories is that fact they will be there when you need some positive reinforcement.

Elvis Presley recorded a simple little song called "*Memories*" (words & music by Bill Strange—Scott Davis, excerpt)

Memories, pressed between the pages of my mind
Memories, sweetened thru the ages just like wine,
Memories, memories, sweet memories

June 29th, 2011, Life seems to be full of lessons. We have had rain forever; the rivers are all in flood stage, some record flood stage. The killer summer heat is coming, more humid because of all the moisture. In the last few years New Orleans was nearly blown and washed away by hurricanes and flooding. Earthquakes and Tsunamis have devastated many countries

It is enough to depress even the happiest Pollyanna. Then when tragedy becomes personal, someone you love disappears; Police seem to be doing nothing. You find that you personally have no control. If you are lucky and find contacts in the world of the missing; If you have support of family and friends; If you have political contacts, then you may be able to find some solace. But reality is you probably won't get help from those who know what happened to your loved one.

This is the situation my family and I find ourselves in. We were fortunate to have a support network, to meet people who could tell us what we could do. But those who could answer our questions are not going to do so; they are the ones who are responsible for our misery.

It would seem no one could stand such abject misery, when you put it all together. Strangely, our situation has some comfort. While we are saddened about the world crises, we have our own to deal with and it lessens the impact of all those huge catastrophes. We have donated to help, but we don't have a lot of time to get depressed, we have a job to do here at home. It is important no matter whom you are that once you become a member of this group, families of the missing, that you reach inside and find the strength to be the representative for your missing. No matter how many or few are there to help, you are the one. We all have to have this vision that we are the answer to getting our loved one back. If I would sum it up in one word, it would be purpose. I remember a Science fiction story in which a man is imprisoned in a darkened room and left in solitude. He survives by taking care of an imaginary mouse. The point of the story is we all need to be needed, to serve a purpose. So while we are feeling sorry for ourselves, we need to go out and find those who may be worse off; Their entire lives may have been filled with misery. You can work at finding your loved one but don't lose yourself in this; Reach out.

Now that I have done you the favor of filling your mind with gloom and doom, I want to say this: With so much misery, that we don't control, it is important that we seek out what ever joy may be found,. Your missing loves you as you love them and they will not want to see your life become one of misery. Purpose, number one, then balance. Balance the good and the bad. Big corporations give classes to their employees on empowerment. Often these classes are not taken seriously. But this is valid way to face challenges in our lives. We must empower ourselves, not wait for mother nature or the police or all those nice people who want to help. We must tap the energy within.

Take these thoughts with you: Purpose, Balance, and Empowerment. Put them together in the right formula and you get Inner Peace. Peace in the world may be a long time coming; but inner peace is a more realistic goal. And if it spreads, world peace might be the result. On a personal level, there are days we can barely get around, Jesse seems to weigh upon us so. But then there are days when his memories and the hope of his return are the buffer that keeps the rest of the world from drowning us in sorrow. Hold tight to the memories, take all the positive energy you can get. The level of Inner Peace you may achieve depends on how well you learn to use all these positives. Anything is possible.

I attended a small church in Georgia, a country church. This was a small, tightly knit congregation; everyone knew everyone. I proposed to the young minister that we start an outreach program, to bring in new people. He had wanted to do that, but did not get a warm response from his members. We held a meeting and he presented the project to the Deacon and other members. The first response of the Deacon was "We saved ourselves, let them save themselves" This from the chosen one, the lay leader of the entire congregation. This was a good lesson for me in making assumptions; And in realizing that we are all a work in progress. Well we were able to bring in some new folks, but the congregation was not very friendly. Not intentionally mean, they just had not developed the habit of thinking beyond their small group. The point I would make is that God grants salvation; no one saves themselves. It is through the mercy of God. He gives us a gift and he expects us to share. One of the couples we brought in was a man and his wife. This lady had suffered burns on her body, not really bad but noticeable. And she was hesitant to appear in public, concerned about what people would say. Here was the perfect opportunity for this church to be a real force of mercy and compassion for God, a example of how his mercy and compassion really works, and we blew it.

So when we are overcome with our special portion of grief and woe that the world dishes out, we need to reach out; Find that person that has a greater need and lose our sorrow in theirs. If you can make your situation better, do it. If you can't then find someone you can help. Who knows maybe fate will bring answers to you while you are bringing answers to others. It is my wish these words will reach someone and make life better for them, thereby enriching my life as well. And we should take comfort in the mercy

God gives to all. Our loved ones may not be perfect, just because we love them, but God loves us all, perfection or not and he is especially there for the victims. Somewhere the bible tells us

"Love Covers a Multitude of Sins" (1 Peter 4:8; James 5:20), So our love may be the salvation of another. I can't say it enough "reach out".

I like to get silly sometimes, so let's do that for a minute. You may be familiar with that country song *I've always been crazy but it keeps me from going insane* . Well being silly once in a while is good. When I was working, we had to provide safety briefings for our work group. I would often pick some presentation with Disney characters comically portraying the hazards of not being safe and responsible. *Goofy* or *Donald Duck*. Someone told me "Safety is serious, you shouldn't be showing cartoons". Well I thought the subject needed some humor, just to keep people interested. So here's my silly.

Let's do our own version of the *Hokey Pokey*. First you reach in(for inner strength) Then you reach out(for strength from others, and to share your strength with them). Grab all your troubles and you shake them all about. Enough . . . . you get the idea. Coping with disaster is not a reflex action(it may seem so with some). It is a determined intentional effort to find the rainbow after the rain.

A minister friend once shared with me that his understanding of the Mormon view of religion was that we existed in heaven, and agreed to spend time on earth, despite it's horrors, and then we would be taken back into glory. It is not my intention to offend anyone, I have no idea if he was right or not. What I would like us to take from this is the idea that we take the earth as it is, and we make the best of it, knowing that someday we will be lifted up.

Those who try to build a permanent place on this earth and are disappointed when some catastrophe occurs and takes it away, need to think about this concept. All through our lives, we see our loved ones pass on., It is a wake up call. No one gets out alive, and no one takes anything with them, except what is in their heart.

Carly Simon sings
"That life is eternal
And love is immortal
And death is only a horizon

So we must cling to the immortality of love, see beyond the horizon.

Surely one of the blessings we can count is music. Our loved ones had music that was special to them; A medium for storing memories of good times. I believe in the eternal nature of memories, especially those born of love. When we are reunited with our loved ones we may share those memories.

Silly time again; I once, described my son's music as the sound of a man in a suit of armor falling down a flight of stairs while the onlookers screamed in the background. I have since revised my opinion somewhat. When I listen to one of Jesse's cd's, I hear his voice speaking to me, "come on dad give it a chance" He loved to spring some new hit on us and get our reaction. "You'll like this one" He'd say. And on occasion he was right. He liked these Irish rebellion ballads and I found them really interesting. Working on really liking them. But he liked some Garth Brooks, and some other music we all enjoyed.

Jesse liked these God-awful (is that politically incorrect, sorry if so) movies of violence and monsters. I probably wouldn't have understood why except I remembered when my mother would walk through the house and we would be watching the people eating plants from Venus or Mars and she would say "That will rot your mind". Maybe it did, but there is still enough left to find something wonderful in the human race and in the life of our son whom we miss more than life itself. The light that shines in our lives comes from our memories of Jesse, from our pride in Andy, our oldest, and all that he has accomplished. From warm moments spent sharing the good times with family and friends.

If you are one of those in need and have not found your light in another, well maybe this is God's way of telling you that you have been chosen to be the light for others. Some of that light will reflect back into your life. Embracing the dark and losing yourself there will solve nothing and will diminish the light for all.

PART TWO

THE PRESENT

(The time at which I actually began to write this book)

CHAPTER 7

2011

July 1st just finished working with my weights. Suddenly the fact I turned 63 on the 27th of last month sinks in. At my age birthdays just come and go. Except for one fact. It means another year older and no closer to Jesse. I read on Facebook someone was excited because they got a new detective on their case and the new guy seemed to be very enthusiastic. We have had maybe six police officials involved and only the first showed any real interest; And that was back four years ago. We have no real contact except form letters every once in a great while, especially if they are getting a little heat from above. So Donna and I have to hope for some great revelation before we pass. Otherwise who will be Jesse's champion? I don't know if Andy will ever come to a point when he wants to do any of the things we do. I often think how sad it would be for a grown mature Andy to be sitting with his children saying "This is your grandfather Don and grandmother Donna whom you never knew. And this is your Uncle Jesse, who disappeared and was never found". Hopefully maybe by then, there would be new technology and/or dedicated detectives who would pursue Jesse's case and then Andy would be saying "Your uncle Jesse will be over later" If you are going to optimistic you might as well be really optimistic.

This brings up one of the important rules for those of us looking for someone. Avoid 'what ifs' (I just shared one with you for the purpose of this book). We can really bring ourselves down if we start speculating about details of what happened to our loved one; or imagining the worst outcome. It is tough for us, we don't know what happened to Jesse and it is easy to start speculating; the media love to hear us do so. "What do you think happened to Jesse?" is a common question. Focus on what you know and can do to get answers that will bring your loved ones home or actually give you answers. "Go toward the light."

Speaking of Light, Sara our dear friend in Grand Haven MI, has dedicated a song '*Let it be*' to Donna and I. It will be played on the 4th of July at the performance of the Musical Fountain, a popular attraction in Grand Haven. This is what I mean when I speak of positive influences. Sara does not have a missing, just a social conscience and a deep affection for others, especially victims. I hear of people who have no family support, apparently no friends. I want to just tell them run and keep running until you find those kind of people. And do not push them away because you are hurting. That is the very reason you need them; we need them.

July 2nd, 2011

My mother often warned us about cats. She grew up believing that if you left a cat with a baby that the cat would suck the breath out of the baby's mouth and it would die of suffocation.

Then I saw a movie about this thing called the incubus.

An incubus (nominal form constructed from the Latin verb, incubo, incubare, or "to lay upon") is a demon in male form who, according to a number of mythological and legendary traditions, lies upon sleepers, especially women, in order to have intercourse with them. Its female counterpart is the succubus. An incubus may pursue sexual relations with a woman in order to father a child, as in the legend of Merlin. [1] Religious tradition holds that repeated intercourse with an incubus or succubus may result in the deterioration of health, or even death.

[2] Medieval legend claims that demons, both male and female, sexually prey on human beings—generally during the night when the victim is sleeping.—Wikipedia

Not quite the same, but as a child I would sometimes wake up struggling to breath and imagining this thing sitting on my chest. Getting up became very difficult; a struggle to get oxygen to the brain and muscles in order to do anything but lie there. I eventually determined on my own that when we sleep in such a way that our oxygen supply is cut off, say lying facedown with your nose in the pillow, the brain begins to create strange images, it does not function well without that life giving supply of oxygen. This morning was like that, I had little desire to rise, thought about just spending the weekend in bed, forget the holiday.

I now believe this 'incubus' has a common name, depression. It comes to us awake or asleep and attempts to rob us of the ability to cope. No demons here, just a trick of the mind. And if you are dealing with a great sorrow or personal tragedy, it often waits around the corner. This is why I believe we need to always be learning always searching for understanding, rather than fearing those things that go bump in the night. Jesse inspired me with his determination. Yes he had his fears, but he overcame them. He pursued his dreams and whatever the result we can take comfort in the fact he faced life head on. Whatever you call it, be aware of this 'incubus' and refuse to be held down; follow your dreams.

Dreamt about Jesse last night. He was a small child and very contrary. I couldn't get him to do anything. I finally decided he must not feel well. Well Jesse did have days like that. Andy was the one who tended to be easy to get along with unless he was feeling bad. That was the first indication of an impending illness. I think again of this 'incubus', blinding me to the fact that something was wrong when the boys were so fussy. When I stopped to think and get some oxygen to my brain, it was clear, that the boys were not feeling well, and sympathy not anger was needed. We read of so many children hurt by impatient parents, or someone's boyfriend or girlfriend. The incubus is us; when we allow ourselves to react without taking a breath and being rational. We have to take responsibility for our own failings.

So when we feel the world on our shoulders, we can know that the answers lie within us. No demons, just a matter of attitude. The original concept of the incubus suggests it was a creation of guilty minds, trying to deal with suppressed sexual feelings. If you broaden that concept, we may find guilt associated with the loss of a loved one and in this case the mind reaches out. Blame the weather, police, that guy who is always posting on the internet. The new 'incubus' has widened his territory. He loves the holidays, anniversary dates, anything that can be used to drag us down. But for us we have a new defense. We now understand that our feelings, our attitudes determine the power of depression(the incubus) to bring us down. It is not always easy to accept this idea, it means we must take responsibility for our actions. But it also means we have control. Let's take Liza Minnelli's advice.

"What good is sitting alone in your room? Come hear the music play. Life is a Cabaret, old chum, Come to the Cabaret".—Liza Minnelli "Cabaret"

Everyday can't be a party, but we can survive on the bad days and we can actually find some joy on the good days. We must realize the answers come from within; First attain inner peace; then peace within the family; someday maybe peace in the world.

Bones, a popular series about a forensic scientist, who works with bones and uses her expertise to help solve crimes, is one of our favorite shows. True it has graphic portrayals of bodies (scheduled right around dinner time) in various degrees of decay, but the human interactions between the characters are the main draw with us. We walk with them through their happiness, sadness, frustrations. I know a soap opera! One of the main characters is Seeley Booth. He is an FBI agent, very outgoing and spontaneous. A former marine sniper, he has learned to control his demons and to stare his fears right in the eyes. He wears a bright red belt buckle that says "Cocky"; A belt buckle and a statement.

I ordered a replica of this buckle. Cost a small fortune, but I didn't just buy a buckle; I bought an attitude. I'm 63 years old. Donna will see this buckle and shake her head. But inside she will know that when I face depression, bad days, I will shine up this buckle and wear it confidently. When depression gets in my face I get in it's face.

I remember working with a lady who retired a few years ago. I would complain about the government agencies that I had to deal with. And she told me her secret. She always manages to be more of a pain to them than they are to her. I told her once about the annoying salesman that called on the phone. She told me she had a cure for that; when they call her she starts telling them about her crazy family and keeps talking until they hang up and don't call back. That lady has no belt buckle, but she has the attitude.

It seems to me that long before many of us were born, gutsy people were pushing their way across this country making it what it is today. They are gone, but they have left a legacy for us; One of courage in the face of depression, and long odds.

126

I once subscribed to the *American Rifleman* a magazine for the NRA. In the front of it were stories of everyday citizens taking the initiative in their own lives? One story was of an elderly lady in Texas. Thugs tried to take her purse, so she spit chewing tobacco in their faces and beat them off with her purse. Okay maybe this is a little extreme, but you see my point. As reverend Dave used to say, "Fight the good fight".

Freedom, democracy, equality. Just words; but associate them with actions and they become extremely important. The way the government works affects us all. If our leaders see these terms as only words then we have no real freedom, democracy, or equality. They must see these terms as real concepts to be applied in our lives.

A word like missing, is just another word unless all of us grasp the significance of what it is like to have someone in our lives go missing. Hopefully the police will think about such things and renew their commitment to our missing loved ones. Perhaps we can help them do that.

July 4, 2011, listened to two versions of America the Beautiful. With all the political controversy, two unpopular wars, illegal immigration, it is often difficult to see the beautiful. As Donna and I traveled to Illinois last month we passed through towns, cities, and farmland. The beauty of America was obvious. Normal Illinois, we stood in the park and watched joggers, passing cars, young couples pushing carriages; People of all races. A beautiful swimming pool, children and adults carrying towels over there shoulders. A couple of ducks swimming in the pool before anyone else got in. A beautiful university just blocks from the park. I subscribe a magazine called *Midwest Living*. A single magazine listing all the wonderful sights to see in the Midwest alone; even with a son missing within the jungle of streets and buildings of Chicago, we still see the beauty of this country; Beauty in its natural resources, its people and its hope for the future.

As far as the controversy, that is another great thing about this country, we may disagree and do so loudly. When there is no more controversy, it means someone has been silenced. It means I can't ask where my son is. You can not state this is unfair or that is unfair. When we see the bright lights in the sky and hear the fireworks all around us, that is the sound of freedom.

Let's all celebrate, what we have now and the hope we have for tomorrow.

I sometimes think it would be easier if my family would draw straws. Then whoever got the short straw would have to spend time at our house. Just a thought. Of course I have had friends tell me they can't get rid of their relatives. We each have our own crosses to bear. Some act as if our house is cursed, bad things happen to those who live here. For us it is a blessing, a place of love and memories to be shared. I wonder if they think Jesse's ghost walks around the place. In a way I suppose it does; but we don't see that at all, we have put as much energy and love into making this a place where people can feel welcome. I guess I watched too much of the *The Waltons* on television, or like Chevy Chase in *Christmas Vacation*, I set standards for people that they can't possibly live up to. Donna is patient and understanding with everybody, especially me. She keeps reminding me what a great family I have and how much I should appreciate them. That is part of the problem, I do appreciate them and look forward to seeing them. I just get a little tired of the one w ay relationship. You can choose your friends but you get your family. At times when I am feeling really selfish, I think I would trade them all for Jesse. Not true, but I do miss him so much sometimes I am not myself. Donna and I watched a sad movie today. Cried together; some for the people in the movie; some for us. We should be grateful we have each other. And all those who are there for us. Holidays can be like this; especially the ones Jesse liked so much.

Anyway I went out bought more fireworks, some noisy ones. Jesse would be so upset if he knew how quiet it was. I suppose being on a Monday, a lot of the people had to work that would otherwise be out making some noise. That's okay; I'll make some of my own. Surprisingly, I miss the guys down the street blowing up toilets. Or the kids who had to use the stuff from their fireworks stand. They turned our street into a war zone. It was so great and so noisy. Jesse was with us then ; I had bought some fireworks, but I think was our first year here and I didn't know how much into fireworks everyone seemed to be. It was special.

Time for a little humor, very little; I was stationed at Fort Bragg NC and did not have a car. My friend had an old Rambler. One day he came over to our barracks; He had an ad for a drive-in movie. If you drove a Chevy you could get into the movie for free. But no one had a Chevy. Finally I suggested we take the Rambler. I was certain there would be a long line of people and a very narrow driveway into the movie. We would just bluff our way thru.

Sure enough we got up to the window and the guy tells us, "That's no Chevy". We looked him square in the eye and told him "yes it is, it's a limited edition, they only made a few of them". He looked at the line of people behind us and realized we couldn't back up or turn around so he let us in for free. Sometimes, you just have to go for it. When the day and the way get you down, don't stand there and frown, just look 'em in the eye and lie; (I know, I'm bad).

Back to the real world, Donna prepared hamburgers, I fired up the grill. My world class problems have not affected my appetite; Great burgers and dogs. I don't believe those who don't eat red meat live longer. I think they just think it's longer. Even if they do I will sacrifice a few years for a good ole greasy burger off the grill any time. I said I was bad!

July 6, 2011, A friend on facebook who lives in Illinois, sent us a link to the Chicago Tribune. Seems they found a body outside of Chicago, a young man lying in a pond. Very unlikely it would be our Jesse, but the possibility exists. We try to ignore these things until there is some sort of verification. But we do appreciate our friends who try to keep us from getting blindsided by the press. One network actually posted a page on the internet saying that Jesse's body had been found (that was some time ago); The worst example of media malice, was when they called on the first Christmas after Jesse disappeared and wanted to sit with us and talk about how we felt. Less than a month after he was missing. Even the press should know what a terrible thing it is to spend Christmas with an empty place at the table. Not something you want to share with anybody. I made an effort to keep things normal, but it was like walking around a 500 lb gorilla sitting in the middle of your living room. I could not give the only gift that we all wanted. I can only advise others to seek the company of family, find strength in the one's who love you.

So for now we wait; Someone will get the bad news. And if not us then we will join with our facebook friends and try to offer some comfort to those affected. We have started a group called Guardians of the missing, A dear friend inspired me to do this. We will try to enlist as many people who have or are resources for the missing.

Got my 'Cocky' belt buckle today, we'll see if I can live up to it.

Had our contractor over to do some work on the house; He has a new partner. They were downstairs looking at the room this contractor had built for Jesse. The new guy kind of did a double take. He told Donna he thought we looked familiar, from TV. This kind of exposure is about all we have, so it is good to know we are reaching people. We can not know just where answers might come from. Plus it is expensive traveling and putting on awareness events, so we look to recruit fans. Our **Opiefest** event generates revenue that helps keep us active through the year. We hate to reduce it all to money, but that is part of the ordeal.

July 7, 2011 Some 'sweet' older lady sent us a message on facebook, all about her conversations with Jesse and descriptions of how he was attacked, about him being in the river, etc. etc. I can not say what this makes me feel. I want to reach out through the modem and strangle this misguided soul. We want to hear that she is bringing him home or nothing. Instead this poor soul who apparently doesn't get enough excitement in her dull life, felt the need to bring sorrow and sadness to us. Donna sees these things and it generates hope, false hope; these parasites apparently have no idea what cruel harm they do to families of the missing; or they don't care. Any ideas people have about our son, unless they are cold hard facts and of some help, then they need to keep those thoughts to themselves. You may have noticed I am a little negative on the subject of psychics, ghost whisperers, mediums, dog psychologists, ghost chasers. Many people are interested in these types, but let me tell you when you have a loved one missing and they start hovering over you with their nonsensical messages you will truly hate them. This is my rant for the day. PS Donna emailed this lady and asked her to contact Chicago Police with her lead or tip. Cooler heads prevail.

I have drafted a letter to the Chicago police department concerning Jesse's case. It should give you an idea of our frustration with the system.

Donald and Donna Ross
xxxxxxxxxxxxxxxxx
xxxxxxxxxxxxxxx

Lt. D
xxxxxxxxxxxxxxx
Chicago, IL 60653

Lt. D,

We are the parents of Jesse Ross, missing in your city since 2006. We are told by your people that Jesse's case is active, yet we have not seen a significant change in Jesse's case in four years. So we don't understand how something that sits on a shelf and goes nowhere can be called active. I know you all have procedures to follow, but we are Jesse's parents. How do you justify keeping us in the dark and simply making some token effort at resolving this case? Since we have been given no part in this, we can only assume nothing is being done. I have seen cases where the only resolution came when someone stumbled over a body. Is this your game plan? We are Jesse's family; The people who love and miss him. Give us something.

His story was just featured on Vanished with Beth Holloway. They interviewed a number of people involved, which is more than your people have done in years as far as we know. Is there not something in this show or the transcripts that you can use to bring some life to Jesse's case;

The Billy Goat Tavern, M, conduct of the school and sponsor, The rave notice. As far as we know no one has looked into any of these matters. We were last told no investigations took place outside the hotel since Jesse had no reason to leave; But we have learned he had motivation to leave for reasons of his career in the music industry.

we are desperately in need of a human being who can feel our pain. So far we have had bland voices on the phone or words in letters assuring us everything is wonderful, and not to call, as we would be called if there was any change(such as stumbling over the body?) I will be in Chicago soon, I hope to speak with you and see if there is some way we can have confidence in a police department of which we hear so much negativity.

Please try to have some kind of meaningful information for us, we will be there this month.

Sincerely
Don and Donna Ross

I don't think most people can begin to believe what it is like to have someone you love and adore, to be treated like some number. If we don't find a way to deal with this then the police become the enemy. Considering they are the only ones assigned the job of finding our loved one, it is not so good to get on their bad side. I think we need to realize that much of the responsibility of representing our missing falls on us. We have to find a way to keep pushing without pushing people away.

Later this month I will partner with someone and travel to Chicago to have a face to face with this detective; see if I can find some way to motivate this detective. I plan on visiting the bar we were told about and will seek a police escort to do so. The last thing I want is to disappear after my son and leave Donna and Andy to go through this all again.

Donna cuts my hair; that is one of those little things that cements a relationship. She has cut my hair as long as we've been married and I trust no one else. This makes me realize the kind of home our sons have grown up in. This is what my wife has brought to our home; a deep sense of love and trust. A place that all of us can come to as a haven from the harshness of he world. A place no one would want to run away from. If Jesse were able he would be here today. Police like to justify their inaction by suggesting Jesse just walked away. Didn't happen and as tough as it may be for us to face, Jesse has been prevented some way from coming home. What is tougher is knowing those who are charged with finding him, are not all that concerned if they do or not. Sunday, July 10, 2011 at 11:28am Those of us with a missing loved one, we try to help others, by sharing what happened. Sharing what we did. But I want to get harsh with myself for a moment. Let's talk about what we didn't do. We didn't keep cool. When our son disappeared we didn't push police. When we hit a dead end we didn't move up the ladder say who is your boss. Police chief, Mayor, Governor. Now I'm not saying these are guarantees, but fact is our son is still missing. perhaps we should not be suggesting people do what we did. It is certainly a monumental task to keep your head and to concentrate on the task as if you were closing a business deal.

But If you don't it is entirely possible no one else will. Think outside the box. I know you may be told police are the professionals, but our experience suggests police don't think outside anything all that well. They might not even be able to find the box. We now know many things we didn't then. We know that there may be individuals and organizations that can help in ways the police can't or won't. Find out the who what and where, much like a journalist.

Find out who in your area represents the media, make some contacts. use your school, church, city govt, do not let anyone tell you that you are required to sit and twiddle your thumbs while daylight burns. *Project Jason* in Omaha was the first solid help we received. *The National Center for Missing and Exploited children*, *Peace4themissing*, and there are a large number online organizations that can help or tell you who to go to. Your missing one is a victim. Don't let yourself be a victim as well. And if you are a family friend or member, take the initiative, those closest to the problem may not be able to do that. My point here is don't let anyone stand in your way. TV cops solve it all in an hour, doing anything and everything, and overflowing with compassion for their victims. This is reality and we may be the strongest hope our loved ones have.

July 10, 2011 mental marijuana that's what I call it. I don't do drugs but we can work on the state of mind. Getting mellow may just involve a change in attitude. In early days they had a day called Sunday, day of rest. You put aside your cares and needs for that day and concentrated on 'getting mellow'. Business's closed down, families gathered for dinners and social time. This practice has all but disappeared as people seek fulfillment from material sources. Run fast enough and maybe it will catch up to you. Today I have chosen to renew the old practice. I'm not reading the news. I will make some plans, but I will not try to meet any deadlines. I will spend some time thinking about Jesse's case, but not trying to implement anything just yet.

July 11, 2011 Steven Knight is a young man who has an internet radio show. I was referred to Steven by a gentleman, whom I met on Facebook. I say met, I have never really met him, I know little about him, but he saw Jesse's story and wanted to help. So I did a phone interview on Steven's show, sharing information and answering questions. Here were two strangers that felt compassion and reached out to us. We are often asked where our strength comes from. Sometimes it is from people we don't even know; there strength is our strength.

July 12, 2011 Today I started the wheels rolling on Opiefest vi. I have reserved the room and will begin to notify those who may want to be involved. Donna is going through her adjustment period; these things are very hard on her; they drain her. I understand this and it is hard for me to put her through this, but I am driven. It is not a case of who loves Jesse the most, it is simply the way we as individuals cope with disaster. Many marriages have dissolved under such pressure. It is difficult, but we keep going.

Speaking of wheels, The *Clementine* band, with Jannel Rap, is starting the *Squeaky Wheel tour* in San Diego CA; We made a donation, but we just can't go to San Diego; Jus t too much on us already. But it is an important event for the missing

There are some good shows on television. Some that cause us to question ourselves. I watched as a man reached into his conscience and found the strength to forgive another for past wrongs. I have seen this at times in real life. Makes me wonder if someday we know about what happened to Jesse and who is responsible, will I have to do some reaching? Listen to the preaching; live the words I have spoken to others? Walk the walk? These are the times when we find out of what we are really made.

July 14, 2011 I have started a support group on Facebook, Guardians of the Missing. My dear friend Kelly J was also part of the group but she had to decline as she is involved in another group and has obligations. Kelly talked with another member about her concerns about this group and some members. I know that in the past she has had some very negative experiences with those who prey upon the families of the missing. This is where misunderstandings are born. I have monitored this group and found no misconduct, but it is open to anyone. I do have standards and I will not allow anyone to use this group to prey on it's members. I think Kelly was disturbed by some names in the group, but since I had no complaints I didn't 'boot' anyone. I do respect Kelly's knowledge and I would err in favor of removing anyone with a past of improper behavior. Apparently Kelly assumed I knew as much about these people as she does. My point being Kelly is a very good friend and resource and it would be silly to start some trouble over a misunderstanding. None of us is perfect and we act in support of each other. I have messaged Kelly and asked for assistance in determining if there are any potential problems. It is my group and I will control it or disband. It. I have seen families come apart over nothing. Jesse his mother and I didn't always agree, but we talked and worked things out. I can at least take some comfort in the fact there were no issues between Donna and I and the son we have missed so dearly these 5 years. The bible tells us to

go immediately and settle our disputes peacefully. This is a
good philosophy for life

July 15, 2011 So hot out today; days like this when it
is so terrible and days of winter when it is so cold, I think
of Jesse and the missing in general. Are they safe from the
weather? So many things to think about; everyday a new
missing. It seems like the world is in a trance. Our loved
ones disappear all around us and no one seems to notice.
I think we all need to start practicing awareness. We need
to watch our children, and all the children. Not trust them
to fate.

July 17, 2011 Downstairs in Jesse's room there sits a
brown decorative wooden box. It is abut 10 by 16 inches. It
contains some things, of little or no value to the world, at
one time valuable to Jesse; now invaluable to us. Following
is the Inventory:

A ribbon for 5th place at the KCPL Invitational track meet
    May 1998
A crucifix
A lanyard that says "Get foul"
A pair of glasses, missing a lens.
A maroon colored wooden box containing a commemorative
    pocket knife featuring a full color picture of the twin
    towers on the side of the knife and top of box.
A Tank Bank gasoline card
A miniature book,' *Absolutely Absorbing Bathroom reader'*
Mid-continent Library 'library' card.
A hand drawn card Tom Petty, 'Ompa Ompa' Willie Wonka
Student ID card UMKC
Fimo black light light bulb holder
Money from some foreign country
Southwestern Bell belt buckle (I gave it to him)

Parking Ticket $38 in my name but incurred by him.

Advertisement for Main St. Café featuring A Dead Giveaway (the band)

Decorative keychain, plastic surfboard, miniature floppy disk keys.

Slightly beat up leather child's wallet with a picture of a deer on the front

Sticker for AFTERBURN recording studios.

Green and Gold O'Hara high school shoe laces

Pages form a Dilbert cartoon calendar

Fraternity button

Card—Plastic surgery 2005 education experience Chicago IL September

Mary J Blige meet and greet Aug 18th 2006 sticker

Hand written note on Sheraton Chicago hotel and towers stationary-notes on speech for model UN conference

University of Kansas post card 2004-5

How to say the Rosary card

Soccer Angel pin

'Passport' from Mrs. Meyers and Mrs. Heringers Spanish class

High School diploma

CD for Netzero service invite for back to school beach party, Sept 17,1989, with picture of Jesse and friends.

Birthday card from Aunt Diane and Uncle Monty

Student ID O'Hara high school, 2003-4

Retainer in box

Decorative wooden letter J\

Golf ball yellow in color

Two ½ tennis balls

Decorative belt buckle with built in pocket knife

Key chain, cloth miniature dachshund attached

Bet buckle with Eisenhower 50 cent piece attached

Knife KU commemorative
Cross Country Medals
Employee ID Dickinson Theatres
Delegate Id Model UN 'China'
Blockbuster membership card
Key ring Buckle up
Drivers permit
Tin with playing cards—World Series Poker
Concert tickets
AMC entertainment card
Runners chest tag #156 from CC or track
A paper 'graduation' cap from primary school
A beer bottle cap-'Beware of Penguins'
Cross Country pin
Mark Davis guitar pick(Brother, of Jesse's best friend, who
    died in a car crash)
Name tag Dickinson theatres
Pro-life bracelet
Plaster model of dachshund
Commemorative knife with picture
Cufflinks from Vietnam (from Uncle Ron to me to Jesse)
An old wristwatch. ***

    Nothing to the world, but treasures to us; Invaluable for the memories attached. And yet as invaluable as they are, we would trade the whole treasure just to know that our son is safe and well, out of harms way. Amazing how some small trinket takes on so much value when you attach it to a person, place, or event. These are not all the things we have left of Jesse, but they are things in which he seemed to place some special value. Some I brought home from trips to Wichita, or California to see my brother. Others sent by family members, still others attached to events we know nothing about. The old faded wallet, important because I remember his wallets, usually thin, short on money, but a few cards, ids etc. Not bragging, just saying it takes great courage to open this treasure chest of memories. But with love comes courage.

Met a young man on *Facebook*, He is dealing with a close friend who has been trafficked out of the country. But he saw our story and hopes to help us. He is in the entertainment industry and knows Chicago. These types of people learn from their need to see the need of others. We regret that we can not be of some help to him. Perhaps the time will come when we can. We both shake our heads at the cruelty of this world.

July 22nd, 2011 It is so hot, heat index is 105. We are going to a dinner tonight with some of my former co-workers who are just getting ready to retire. It will be nice to see some of the familiar faces; reminders of a time before 'missing' became such a huge part of our lives. A time when going to work was our biggest headache. Again bittersweet, but we have to take all the sweet we can get. . Jesse was my main man on the riding mower. He knew how to get the little trouble spots, without even dismounting from the mower. I was out this morning replacing the solenoid, so I was mowing in the late morning heat. Neither of our boys seemed to mind the heat, while my favorite place is in front of the ac. Our contractors are working on our basement; they are glad they can be in from the heat. They are also friends so we are glad as well. We have to wonder, if Jesse were around, where he would be. Education behind him maybe looking for work; maybe even in Chicago; Chicagoans may not realize they just lost a valuable resource.

July 23rd, 2011, Thinking abut Time Warner, tells me they can't work on our internet problem for six days. . It' not their fault I guess, they don't' realize that an important part of our day is spent on the internet, looking for anything about Jesse; or about some other families missing. This is our primary communication link with those who make up our support network; We get our daily boost of hope. So six days of famine. I suppose I could have told them our story, but I guess I feel like every customer should get good service, not just those who are in our situation.

Yesterday, was nice. We braved the heat and met at a little sports bar called the Brooksider, just off 63rd street and Brookside plaza. It was noisy and crowded.

People started showing up about the time we did. Some still on the job; some retired; All with stories. Some who battled cancer and other illnesses and won. Some are grandmothers, doing volunteer work, others looking out for the grandkids. Then some like us, retired, doing some travelling seeing friends; Proving a job is just a job, but life is so much more. So our story, touching as it might be, is just another. One lady has lost a son to a car accident. Reminds us we still have hope for this life. Also reminds us we all have hope for the next one. If we don't have the promise of life beyond this, what do we have?

I am also reminded that I don't miss the job, but it is nice to see the familiar faces. I will take this time to preach a little. Those of you just starting out or somewhere along in your career, think about the years to come. Don't let yourselves get stuck in a job that you can't afford to leave when the time comes. It is tough putting money back for the future; seems our government doesn't' sympathize much. But we really have to take care of ourselves and prepare. It is easy to procrastinate, but the time comes sooner than we realize.

July 24th, 2011 "Some broken hearts never mend"—Don Williams. I dreamt that I was going to school. Not attending school but just hanging around some college or university and waiting for a class to start, then sitting in. No one seemed to question why I was there. I was leaving a building, one story, with glassed walls and a set of glass double doors to exit. I walked out the doors and I stopped and turned to look back. As I did a tall slim young man was going in the doors. He stopped, turned and looked at me; It was Jesse. I called out to him, but he just turned and entered the building. As it is in dreams, my feet were stuck in place and I couldn't follow, just stand there and call his name. I then dreamt that I was crying and Donna woke up. She tried to comfort me. When I actually woke up l realized Donna was sleeping peacefully. I was glad. I didn't want to share this with her and reopen the wound in her heart. I wanted to share this with my supporters on Facebook, but thanks to Time Warner, I am unable to do that. They ran a commercial yesterday about how they have such great their customer service. Sayin' and doin' two different things. I will leave you all to feel what you may about this company, I am just expressing my feelings. Maybe in a week or two I will not be so down on them. We'll see. It would seem I would want to share my deepest thoughts with the one closest too me; But I can not bring myself to pass on this deep and terrible emptiness to my wife. I guess I feel like this is one of the valuable things about the people we have met online. They are more than happy to help shoulder such burdens. In truth I am happy to shoulder the burdens of others. Their burdens, for me, are much lighter as mine are for them. Dealing with our own sorrows is much more difficult than to face those of others; And vice versa.

July 28th,2011 Clouding over, a little cooler today. I was charging the battery on the riding mower and big fat rain drops started to fall; Really tired of the heat. My brother and his wife did a hit and run yesterday; they do that a lot, blink and you miss them. Spent some quality time with the neighbors, just laughing and joking, learning some history of their family; Family is so important few realize just how important. Until one is lost then it opens the eyes to what we had. Hopefully we can then learn to appreciate the ones left to us, even the ones who just hit and run.

I have learned word processing is an abstract art. Words, sentences, paragraphs and pages disappear before your eyes; Or duplicate. You think you are typing on page 5, but somehow, you are actually inserting text for page 5 on page 7. You scroll through pages and find there is more than one copy of a page, of a number of pages. But generally what is lost is usually recoverable; Wish I could say the same for missing sons. Of course there is still hope for us, but 5 years is oh so long.

July 29th,2011 We had dinner at our favorite Mexican place, *Mi Pueblito*, with Jim and Rhonda, the parents of Kara Kopetsky who disappeared here in Belton, shortly after Jesse disappeared. We enjoy their company and share information on our particular cases. When we start feeling bad because Chicago is so far away and our case seems so hopeless, we remember that Kara disappeared right here in Belton. We need to realize there are others in our situation who still wait and hope and their circumstances are different than ours. So we can take hope that all cases have one thing in common; Hope. Jim and Rhonda involve themselves in local activities that help keep Kara in the public eye. We both agreed it can be frustrating because the media looks for excitement and novelty. They often would rather print some silly article on some obnoxious celebrity than to do real investigative reporting. Asking key questions of police; For example what progress has been made on a case? Why hasn't progress been made? What other agencies are involved? And perhaps creating a report card, to show whether police are doing a good job and if not how they can improve. Just today I read a new report an 11 year old girl, just gone missing.

Despite our many common concerns, we find the time we spend with Jim and Rhonda to be relaxing and a comfort. A mariachi band strolls by and we ask them to play *Cielito Lindo*, about the only Spanish song I know. It has become a tradition for us when we gather at *Mi Pueblito*. The Beckford's are always in our prayers as well when we think of Jesse.

Saturday, today, we go to 4:30 church. Tomorrow we gather with family, to remember the son not here, and to celebrate the one that is here.

Sunday July 31st, 2011, we met with family at Donna's folk's place; Lots of eating and talking and sharing. Donna's sister from Oregon was in, so gave her a Jesse bracelet. I have a great pic of her and Jesse when he was little. We will share that with her. We have made plans for the whole week before Sis goes back to Oregon. Time with these people is like an antidote for the dark feelings that often come when we get frustrated with the lack of progress in Jesse's case. On facebook we read of a missing found safe; Another found floating in a lake. We have to focus on the positives and minimize the negatives. We send our happiness to one, our condolences and prayers to the other. We cherish those that are still here with us, and hold dear those that aren't.

August 3, 2011, Carole Moore has written a book called *The Last Place You'd look.* I am currently reading this intriguing volume.

I read about those caught in the web of mental illness or some form of addiction, and the fact they are often not considered worth the time of law enforcement, compared to other 'missing'.

I think 'what if my son somehow got pulled into this group'. What if he is wondering the streets somewhere, unrecognized because no one cares enough to look at these people, as though they are no longer human. So many possibilities, they are all torture to those who wait and hope. If we could somehow transfer the terrible pain we all feel, into the hearts of those who are responsible for bringing the missing home, perhaps they would be more motivated to find those who are loved by someone.

In Nov 2006 your organization was prepared to put us on national television about our missing son Jesse Ross. You instead went with the terrible weather that afflicted the east and midwest. Understood. But we feel you all sort of owe us something; If not us then Jesse. He is still missing after 5 years and we need some big guns in our corner to get the Chicago police to do anything. Please take compassion on us and Jesse. Thank you. Donald Ross.

The above paragraph is text from an email I sent today to Fox and one of their big national shows. Once in a while I get an inspiration. Sure these folks may completely ignore us, but maybe not. We have to acknowledge that they are a business, but we can also hope for some human compassion to come into play. Or someone is thinking maybe ratings as well as human interest. We do what we have to do.

We often draw comfort from the routine, especially when we get older. Favorite television shows, books, places and faces fill us with warmth. Those of us with a missing are much the same as others, but sometimes the routine is torture; Another weekend and no clues. Our loved one is still gone and no one has a clue. So the routine is a hateful thing; we long for change, some kind of progress; a call from police telling us they have a lead. We are slowly being buried in routine, and those who are charged with finding our loved ones, they have their routines. We long to see them move beyond those routines and do something different, out of the norm. Criminals are always doing something unpredictable, based on their knowledge of the predictability of those who pursue them. Sometimes doing all you can do, is not enough, you much reach.

August 5, 2011, Sometimes we are VW's ; Sometimes we are Humvees. Just human, nothing more nothing less, that is what we are. Why might this be important? If you have a missing, there will be times when you plow through brick walls. This can be a dangerous practice, but it has it's upside. All that adrenaline helps keep us on our feet and moving. Those VW days can be a challenge as well. It is easy to get down, to just wallow in the sorrow that has become part of our lives. Our guard is down, and we are vulnerable. So there are times when we just need to make it through the day, nothing grandiose. *Opiefest* will be in November; Now I am beginning preparations. Just crossing T's dotting I's, routine stuff.

Thing is routine is a big part of life. We have to learn to deal with it as much as we learn to deal with the exciting stuff. Routine can undo you. When we are before the crowd we can feed on their energy and hope. But when we sit alone, working on some small detail (planning an event), we are susceptible to depression, loss of hope, fatalism. Call this a heads-up, not just for families of the missing, but any who are dealing with personal tragedies. Be aware and keep some reserve inside to sustain you. And do not expect to move mountains every day. You may be the army that is fighting for your loved one and you are important and needed, even on the slow days.

Donald Ross

With _Opiefest VI_, I have found a routine. Now it is up to me to make it more than just routine. Five times those who love Jesse have gathered; and five times we have seen no real progress in Jesse's case. So how many times do we gather: One more than the last time. **Never ever ever give up**; this is from a poster; but we need to write it on our hearts.

August 7ᵗʰ 2011, I recall a story from high school, _The Monkey's paw_. This is the story of a couple, in need of money, who accept a talisman from an old friend. The monkey's paw, a mummified monkey's hand, with the purported power to grant wishes is used by the couple to wish for money. They soon realize the curse of the paw as they gain money and lose their son. Desperate, they wish again for the return of their son, only to find the paw has returned some horrible thing from the grave that is not their son any more. They wish the thing back into the grave and vow never again to ever use the paw. I thought of this story today; what terrible evil might we unleash in our desperation to see our Jesse again? A world full of people looking for someone and we think we are privileged that we might use some dark force to achieve what God has not thus far deemed to be.

I cannot say what should be or not, but It would be selfish to wish my son back and not think of all the others also in need. Somehow we must deal with our grief and be strength to others also dealing. The end of this week we will go to the Retreat for the Missing, sponsored by _Project Jason_. We will share the experience with others and perhaps find some temporary relief in sharing of our sorrow with others who are where we are, or maybe just starting out on this highway of tears. God grant us all patience.

August 11ᵗʰ, 2011 preparing to go to Omaha tomorrow for retreat for the missing; always some mixed feelings when we are doing Jesse things. We are looking forward to seeing Kelly and company; but it also dredges up a lot of issues. At least we will be in the company of those who are experts at dealing with such things; and we will be there with some folks who are just where we were four years ago.

Andy sent me an email. There is a Star Trek convention in Chicago the end of September. Andy and Jesse and I, over the years, have attended many of these. We have accumulated trading cards, toys, action figures, model starships, and magazines. I look at a toy and remember a Christmas or a birthday. Moments shared.

August 13, 2011, At the retreat, it is now Saturday, we arrived last night and had introductions, told our stories and got to know each other. Today learning sessions begin.

At retreat found this book:, *Thank My Lucky Scars* by Ward Foley, aka Scarman; Ward was a featured guest at this years retreat. His life story makes us feel somewhat ashamed of the times we are lost in our own problems. And yet the overall effect of this person is to leave you laughing and feeling uplifted. He shared his experiences, the obstacles that life put in his way, from birth onward. And he shared the positive outlook that helped him make his life meaningful, in service to others. I recommend this book and I recommend speaking to Ward in person, he will truly enrich your life

This is our 3rd retreat for Project Jason, and it is amazing how much we have learned each time. Dealing with a missing loved one is an ongoing process and each retreat has been a boost for us, a chance to recharge our batteries. It is a dynamic experience, constantly changing, giving new insights. Those whom we encounter bring their on perspective and story to the mix. I urge anyone carrying the burden of a missing or recovered loved one to consider this experience. You will meet strong caring people, individuals who have been there. You may learn from them and they will learn from you.

For Donna and I this was a chance to meet with old friends, encounter new friends and refuel for the coming months. Carrying our burden takes a toll even when we have learned techniques for coping. So we stop along life's road and break bread and get a surge of energy; A hug, a few tears, some smiles and a renewed sense of purpose. In any difficult situation we must first take care of ourselves, and then look to the needs of those around us. Laughter does so much for us; If we forget how to laugh, our burdens are multiplied. All this may seem a bit much to take in, but like anything else, it is one step at a time. Firstly we must just realize that there is hope, we just need to reach out and not be afraid to share our sorrow.

One of the important revelations we discovered: Sometimes those closest to us may not be the ones we depend on; Not always, but sometimes we find the company of those who have been where we are, to be more helpful. Now, we do not drop the old friends because we have new ones, but I think we have to recognize different people cope with loss in different ways. Do not put too high expectations on others. They will probably be there for us as much as they can. Trying to change those around us to meet our expectations can add another burden to the one we already have.

Kelly J covered the *Project Jason* website. If you have a missing one, you may join the site and have available to you, many resources. *The Healing Harbor* allows access to a wonderful therapist. *The forum* allows you to input your own information and to see information concerning other members. It is a good place to explore and seek help.

We joined together at the beautiful chapel just a short drive from the retreat. This modern glass structure sits high on a hill top overlooking highway 80 and the surrounding country side.

There we had a candlelight service to honor our missing loved ones. As I sat and enjoyed the service, Kelly's niece singing hymns, the alter decorated with photos of our loved ones, I was struck by a sad thought that Donna and I might someday be sitting in a church for Jesse's funeral. This is part of the reason his being 'missing' is so tough; because we know that even if/when he is found it may not be over.

Still I was able to appreciate the moving service. The sun was going down; there was a golden hue in and around the beautiful chapel. We were there with our thoughts of Jesse and our retreat 'family'. All gathered to support and care for each other. Also to pray for the return of all precious loved ones. There was a great diversity in the group surrounding us, but a single purpose. Many persons, but one heart.

August 18, 2011 A night of Jesse dreams.

dream 1

I dreamt I was sitting at my desk in the downstairs of a house. Not this house but my house in the dream. I was very content and happy. Little Jesse comes running down the stairs crawls into a closet. It is like there is standing closet in the middle of a divided hallway. He crawls in and pulls things over him to hide. Andy comes running down and I see he is not happy. I ask what is wrong and he tells me about he latest bit of orneriness Jesse has been up to. I pull him close and give him a hug. Donna appears and she tells me she is taking the boys somewhere so I give them both a hug.

dream 2

Andy and I are at a group meeting, like scouts, or something. He points out a tall young man who is disguised. It is Jesse. We are both excited. We go to the young man but he does not recognize us. We lose him in the crowd; but we hunt until we find him. His hair is white. He looks ill used. He tells me he is afraid to come home. I pull him close to me and tell him not to worry he is home. There is a counsel of some sort and they make some judgment against Jesse. But I go to each of them and I say You can not judge him, if you do not judge me or yourselves for he is no different than we are.

August 30th, 2011 Detective O. from Area 3 SVU, Chicago police, called today. He wanted to share a tip he had received from the *Vanished* episode. Some one thought they saw Jesse in Florida, but it was a false alarm. He also asked what new information we had if any. This is the first time we have had anyone ask us for our input in years. I gave him information about the Lifetime show, about some of the people that the show's producers had turned up. He had not seen the show and I don't think he possessed the knowledge that others assigned to Jesse's case has previously made known to us. Still he is young and seems interested in the case so we will try to cooperate. Things just seem to come out of the blue. Of course it could have something to do with the postcard I sent to the Belmont station in Chicago. These are the actual detectives that work the case, opposed the admin people we have been targeting in the past. Hope comes in many forms so we will look for some good here. I know it must be difficult to work with families of the missing, but it is equally hard to be a family of a missing person.

September 1ˢᵗ, 2011, Bryce and Jesse from A Dead Giveaway stopped by for a pre-Opiefest meeting. We exchanged ideas and talked about the structure and the preparation for this event. Bryce just returned from traveling to many locations over the globe. Jesse explained about his whiffle ball injury

Watching these two sit in our kitchen and snarf down pizza, I think about Jesse and how wonderful if he could be here with his friends. I see the lives that Jesse's friends have made for themselves and I can't help but wonder what he would be doing now if only things were different. That little big word again, 'if'.

The band members will lend their talents to our awareness event for Jesse for this year. It is special because they are not actually a band anymore, but will be for this event. Who can say what is in store for these wonderful young men, but Jesse will be a common bond for them for all their lives.

Sept 8ᵗʰ, 2011 To date, we informed our pi of the call from Chicago police. He informed us he had already shared all the information the Detective was asking him to provide. He agreed to call and try to get some kind of action from Chicago. I begin to think this call was merely a move to placate us and keep us quiet for a while. I have heard nothing concerning the new information from the broadcast of Jesse's story on *Vanished*. Nor have the police indicated that they will pursue interviews with M in Michigan or any other former students that were with Jesse. Donna and I will see someone face to face in a few weeks, in Chicago to ask why they aren't doing anything. 5 years and people forget. 5 minutes, 5 years, 5 decades and we can not forget that terrible day.

Sept 11th is just around the corner; the terrible 10 year anniversary of the attacks on the twin towers, the pentagon, and the attempted attack on the Whitehouse. We must put aside our small problem for that day and embrace those who lost and were lost. Our own private hell is eclipsed by a world encompassing disaster. There is some good in everything. I think back to that Sept; Donna, the boys and myself were at South Padre Island, enjoying the company of other family and the tropic beauty of South Padre. I remember Jesse and I walking to a nearby bar, in hopes of seeing the Kansas City Chiefs play. He was really too young to be in the bar, but this being a tourist Mecca, He was allowed to enter with me just to watch the game. Their were several games on various televisions and people from all over were watching their favorite teams. They cheered when we entered, seeing Jesse's bright red Chief's jersey. The Chief's did not win, but everyone had a great time; We met others from Kansas City as well. We will join all those who mourn and recognize the significance of Sept 11th; But we will also carry the fond memories of that time when we were whole, When we felt so lucky during a time when so many others were hurting. We can't know what is to come, so cherish and hold your loved ones close.

Sept 11th, 2011,Chiefs played again, still did not win. Went to church to spend time with our spiritual family. *Facebook* is full of 9/11 related news. A very quiet Sunday for us. Reminds me of when John Kennedy was shot. Seemed like the weekend would never end, countless hours of watching video, glued to the set unable to do anything else. Hearing about the first responders and their many medical problems due to their rescue efforts. Government needs to take care of these brave people.

Sept 22nd, 2011 Thursday, received a call this week from Chicago police. The local CBS affiliate in Chicago wants to run Jesse's story. Not so unusual to hear someone wants to run Jesse's story, but unusual to get a call from the police. We are just happy to get some attention for Jesse. They also want to send a local crew here in Kansas City to do some taping at our home. Been there, so we are again glad they want to come. Next week we will be in Chicago then on to Michigan for some r & r (rest and relaxation) with friends. Wanted to see M who was in Chicago while there, but she is hard to pin down. Maybe there are still people who don't want to talk about Jesse. If they knew what it meant to us just to learn some new detail of what went on in Chicago when our son was so far away, maybe they would be more willing to share. Left a message for Detective O, letting him know our plans. Haven't heard back. Will have to make some more calls, especially if the press will be there(they want to meet us at the police station on Belmont).

September 26th, Here we are in Bloomington IL. Staying in Days Inn. Last night did not sleep well, strange dreams. Tomorrow at 2:30 P.M. we will meet with police and press. Got a long list of questions. Big one is what are they going to do to find our son? This one day will be stressful; then on to Grand Haven MI for some rest. There are days when it seems we are alone and other days when it seems we have an army of support. Friended on *Facebook* another young lady who was with Jesse in Chicago. She hasn't responded. Found an email account with UMKC, sent an email. I think we are a pain to some, but we will try anything for our son's benefit. Kansas City has a new all comedy radio station. It's funny, but today on the internet site, they were telling a joke about a missing person. The punch line of the monologue was "*they found her in a shallow grave. Where else would she be? They should have looked there first.*" This is humor? I sent an email to the station program manager asking if this was appropriate. Guess I understand why some comedy is not funny to all of us.

September 27, 2011, Up early, motel breakfast. I realize how hard this is for Donna. I generally have a driving obsession that propels me along. But I think for Chicago and the frustrating process of dealing with police who know nothing but don't want to admit it, is stressful beyond words. So we will get past today and relax in Michigan. Hopefully we will mend some fences and get some kind of knowledge from our visit. Appropriately today is chilly and overcast. We are 2 and a half hours or so from Chicago. Time to relax a bit and plan strategy. Donna has prepared questions and requests for action. We will see what happens.

September 27th, 2011 1100pm We spent about 2 and a half hours with police. They were polite, told us Jesse's case was active but suspended, meaning they would only act if someone else brought them information. We were encouraged to pursue our own investigation and to present them something definite that they could work on. They did give us a copy of a picture of Jesse outside the conference hotel, talking on his phone. At least we know where we stand and we have met the two persons responsible for Jesse's case. They will not be re-interviewing or doing anything except working clues that others bring to them. They did arrange for Jesse's story to be aired on CBS channel 2 in Chicago. We have no details as to the title of the show, but understand it will air in a day or so.

October 9th, 2011 Got back from Michigan the past week, Monday night. The time spent in Chicago was mostly frustrating, trying to find the police station; talking with the detectives about their plans to do nothing. We had hoped to see our new friends in Michigan, but they are having a baby soon and I don't think things were going well. It was mostly cold and wet in Grand Haven, but we had a great time. Visiting lighthouses, shopping in all the cute little shops, and eating out. The lake was beautiful and wild. There were windsurfers and surfers. I picked up some books on local lore. The Inn where we stayed is run by a really nice couple, Mike and Linda. Made us feel really at home.

It was nice to get back home, focusing on finishing our basement and back to matters of Jesse. The police promised to send us some personal items of Jesse's that we had sent to them for possible fingerprints. They had the items for months and never did anything with them. So we have been trying to get them back, but now fear police may have lost them. We will keep writing and calling until they tell us what they have done or will do

October 10th, Today I slept until 2:00 pm unable to leave my dreams, unwilling to face the quiet of our house, despite the fact it is our home. I think I miss the noise, when the workman were down in the basement making noise and clomping up and down the stairs, it was like having our son back in the house; Their youth and wild and crazy ways bringing back the feeling of completeness when we had Jesse here. I miss all that and the quiet weighs on me. Donna was down in the basement painting and I was getting ready to type all this, and the doorbell rang. It was some pretty young woman, selling magazines. I have read about these companies; They are like slave shops, offering jobs to young people and barely paying them anything while harassing them to make sales. I didn't buy anything, but she saw our poster for Jesse on the door and asked about him. I explained about our situation. She felt really bad and cried and gave me a big hug. I warned her about the dangerous world out there and about taking precautions when out alone. She was 20, a year older than Jesse when he disappeared. I worry for all the young people out in this too too hostile world.

October 12, 2011 3:30 am, I awoke with tears in my eyes. I had the most vivid dream. I was at some school event. Jesse's friends and faculty members were there. I talked with some of them and they assured me they had seen Jesse there. I knew that he was going to want to hang around, it was like one of the carnivals where I had spent time as a young man and I knew he would want to be on his own. But I felt uneasy and I wanted to see him. Mr. K was there, family friend and Jesse's friend, soccer coach, and all-round great guy. Of course I should have wondered about that, in real time Mr. K had passed on unexpectedly and could not have actually been there. I began to realize, in my dream that I was sort of living out those last days when I was actually home in Belton MO, while Jesse was in Chicago. Dreaming on, Jesse appeared out of the crowd, and he had that distracted look in his eyes, just like I remember the very last time I saw him before he left for Chicago; when I drove away without being a parental bore and let him have his adventure with his friends. In my dream, I told him to have fun, I pulled him close and gave him a big hug, told him I loved him. I got a little teary-eyed and my voice broke. I could see he was thinking "now don't go all nursing home on me". I told him please be careful, but I let him go, knowing I might not see him again. It was my job as a parent to get out of the way. My heart was breaking, but I let him walk away. As if I could have stopped him in my dream world, knowing dreams have their own agenda.

I awoke then, feeling as if I had really touched him; the features of his face exactly as I remembered them. The experience so real I could not shake my feelings of loss; And yet feeling as though I had just received a precious gift, if only for a moment. A Heaven sent gift from Mr. K and maybe Jesse, offering what comfort they could; What sweet, sad things dreams can be.

I think back to the young lady at my door, asking about Jesse; shedding a tear and giving me a hug. And the lady at the lumber store earlier today, asking about my Jesse button and sharing a little sympathy upon hearing Jesse's story. Maybe this was the seed for my dream. I'm asking no questions, just grateful for that moment.

October 13th, 2011 a friend sent us a Facebook message, someone had found some bones in a basement, just blocks from where Jesse disappeared. No word from the police, but a friend of ours who is a reporter in Chicago let us know they determined it was animal bones. We are so thankful it wasn't Jesse or any other family's missing.

October 15th, 2011 Helen who is a friend from the missing retreat, has just learned the body of her missing mother has been recovered. It is terrible when you spend your life waiting and hoping and then you must go thru the sorrow all over again when something like this happens. It is a double tragedy. Helen is a bubbly outgoing young woman and her husband just returned from a tour of duty overseas. It is good her husband is now home, to help her deal with her loss. We grieve also, Helen is part of our family, our family of the missing, and always shall be.

October 22, 2011, we are going over to the Kansas side to help put up posters for another family with a missing son. He disappeared in Olathe KS. Would like to do for them what we can't do for ourselves. Called Chicago police, they let me leave a message as usual; Sent a postcard asking Det. O. to send Jesse's personal effects, been asking for months. I think they have lost these things and don't want to admit to it. When you sit down and talk with these detectives, they seem sort of cocky know it all's; Doesn't explain why they know nothing after 5 years.

We arrived in Olathe around 1 pm. There was a handful of people including the parents of Ryan Bradley (missing since Oct 9th, 2011), on hand. We separated into small groups,(our dear friend Maureen Reintjes was there), and set out to place poster's in the nearby businesses. Looking and listening to Ryan's parents was like seeing ghosts of ourselves. Even with our concerns about Jesse, I couldn't help but feel a sense of hope that this young man would turn up and the family would be spared the sorrows that we have endured thru the years. A victory for one is a victory for all. Not that this lessens our desire to see our Jesse home again. We endure what we must and we take the good as it comes to us. With Jesse disappearing so far away, we find hope in the fact Ryan was living in the area in which he disappeared; perhaps the family can generate some local interest and find some answers. The late comedian and motivational speaker Jerry Clower would tell the story of a man hunting raccoons, who finds himself sharing a tree with an enraged Lynx (like a bobcat). He yells down to his friends "just shoot up here amongst us, one of us has got to have some relief." That's how we feel; some of us have got to have some relief.

October 27, 2011, Today we received Jesse's personal items from Chicago police. Hoping our PI will be able to get some use out of them(maybe lift some fingerprints). Andy, our oldest was supposed to be here today, but apparently he forgot several major projects. I was really irked and chewed him out on facebook. Sometimes I feel like I have lost two sons. I seem to remember I was not very responsible in my first years away from home, so maybe this is payback. I talked to Donna about taking in a college student, just to have some kind of activity, it gets really quiet around here; But she doesn't want to; My sister and her husband took in foreign exchange students and seemed to enjoy the experience. I guess this isn't my day. Think I'll find a quiet corner and sulk, maybe miss Jesse for awhile.

October 31, 2011, Halloween is here. But then we have a haunted house all year. Haunted not by what is here, but what is not. Tomorrow we will go up to Lincoln NE to be with recording artist and family of the missing member Jannel Rap. She will be there to honor her missing sister Gina Bos(along with others), who disappeared from Lincoln, NE in October of 2000. Tomorrow is also November 1st, 18 days to *Opiefest* and 21 days until the 5th anniversary of Jesse's disappearance. Five doesn't seem like a big number, but when you are talking about years, it is forever.

November 1st, 2011, Nov 1st and it is 70+ degrees outside. Sitting in the Super8 motel in Lincoln NE. Donna and I are waiting to go to *Dietze's music house,* to see Jannel Rap and co. This is part of the *Squeaky Wheel tour* to recognize and aid the missing and their families. These things always leave us with a knot in our stomachs. We are glad to have the support, but it unfortunately is a reminder of the reality of our situation. Kelly Jolkowski will be there, so we will know someone. Jannel is a friend, but we have never met her except online. The whole thing is like a school play, exciting but nerve-racking. We are here so Jesse is here, he is one of those being officially remembered.

Back at the motel. We spent a great time with Kelly Jolkowski, Jannel Rap, various local musicians and general guests. The music was great, some of us were allowed to speak about our missing loved ones. Jannel and crew have a busy schedule lined up for the coming days. Great exposure for the missing. And we got to share Jesse with a new audience. Will have to wait and see if anything new comes up.

November 2nd, 2011 Woke up at 4:30 am. I had this image in my head, a picture of Jannel Rap on a background like a page from a photo album. Then I remembered in my dream I saw myself like Jannel but It was not a flat picture, but a box. I spent the rest of my night trying to get my brain to rest. I started thinking. We all often find ourselves in a box. We think all we can have or be is in that box. But Jannel and Kelly Jolkowski are two people that saw beyond the box. They took their tragedies and they expanded their world in order to make things better. Then they helped others, like Donna and I to break free of our boxes. You can not limit yourself if you seek to achieve all that is possible. Our Jesse went beyond the box. He took chances to fulfill his dreams. Some will see his disappearance as all negative. But we must be prepared for adversity when we pursue our dreams. And ultimately we will all break free of another box. We will leave behind or physical limitations, the pain and sorrow and can't do's of this world and discover our true potential. True it is not without risks, but we do not walk alone.

For those who can't see beyond the box, it is up to the rest of us to be there. All that talk about brotherhood and peaceful co-existence is real. It is the only hope of the future. Never ever ever give up.

November 6th, 2011, Started reading John Walsh's book *TEARS OF RAGE.* I was not really familiar with the details of the story. Reading about the details leading up to Adam's abduction, I am reminded of a time with Andy when he was small and riding in a shopping cart, while I pushed it around in Walmart. I stopped the cart and stepped around the end of a row of shelves to look at something, and when I had stepped back to the cart, a very stern, disapproving woman wearing a Walmart vest told me "That is just about how long it takes for someone to take a child." Now you might think I would have been mad at this woman. Maybe jumped on the defensive. Instead I felt a coldness in the pit of my stomach and I realized how right she was. I thanked this woman and I will tell you I don't know her, but I still love her. She told me what I needed to hear.

Reading about the life of John Walsh and family, I realized this man had a great life. He was blessed in many ways, so much happiness. Many people in the world will never know or have what this man had. And they seem to me to be a wonderful family. They were careless for just a few moments and some lowlife scum turned their beautiful world into a nightmare. I am not in control of the world, but I will truly never understand how such terrible things can happen to people who are just living their lives; harming no one; Loving and caring for those around them. My wife and I are different from the Walsh family in many ways; our lifestyles vary greatly; But we share a number of characteristics. We were happy just to be a family, to see our children grow up safe and sound. Materially the Walsh family was in a class far above ours; but they were not obsessed with wealth; they had it but their main focus was on living life and enjoying what they had, especially family and friends. John's love for his son rings true to the joy I feel as a father and husband. Here you have two families cruising thru life, seeing a world of joy and love and then suddenly we are both brought to the realization that evil is everywhere and no one is beyond it's reach. The Walsh family is Catholic; so are we. It is my hope that their faith sustains them as ours has for us.

November 10, 2011, I am reminded of an old joke.

A man is wandering around under a streetlamp, looking at the ground. A friend of his happens along.

"What are you doing?" asks the friend.

"I lost a quarter, I'm looking for it." The man replies

The friend starts to look also.

Pretty soon the friend asks: "Where did you lose it?"

"Over there", the man points out into the darkness.

The friend scratches his head and asks:

"If you lost it over there., why are looking over here?"

The man replies "Because the light is better over here."

Stay with me readers, there is a method to this madness.

I read a news story of a man who was robbed while overseas. He waited until he got home to report the theft. He was asked why he waited so long. He told the local police that he felt they would do a better job of investigating the crime than some foreigners he didn't even know.

Okay there is a point here; Donna and I met with our friend Mary Lou last night. She is a driving force in the planning and development of Opiefest, our annual awareness and fundraiser for Jesse's case. So Jesse disappeared in Chicago, but here we are 'looking' in Kansas City. Our support group is 'better' here. Perhaps we should be in Chicago braving freezing temperatures and savage winds, struggling against mother nature and calling Jesse's name as we go. Again I am reminded of the young lady's comment last year "Why are you having parties when you should be looking for your son?" If you have ever been to Chicago, you know what a monumental task it is trying to find anything even in good weather. Or handing our flyers to people who sympathize but really have no clue what they are supposed to do. And there are those 'foreigners we don't even know', the Chicago police, who don't seem to know what to do either. I guess the answer to why we are 'looking over here' is that there is a light; A light that radiates from the familiar faces and places of home. We find frustration in Chicago and friends and family here. So we raise awareness for Jesse and money for the expenses involved when we do go to Chicago, or some place in Illinois, or where ever we get a chance to talk about Jesse. Also for buttons, for postcards, for posters and petitions to keep Jesse in the public eye. We have a public and a private eye working for our benefit. This may be surprising to most of you, but police play a very small part in our hope of finding Jesse. This doesn't mean they won't find him, but they really don't care to have family members 'nosing' around in their investigation, such as it is, so we must have our own.

It is now almost 2 am. When we have these planning meetings for Opiefest or when we travel to other related events, it is like having our heads submerged in the whole terrible experience again. But it is something we must do. The little girl asking about 'parties' does not know the anguish that comes with having to face the terrible reality of our lives without Jesse, when we are involved in these 'parties'. They drain us physically and mentally. When we talk with our 'missing' friends they too know what we are going thru, they suffer the same feelings with their missing loved ones. So we meet we plan and then we get home and the subconscious mind goes into action. When we lie down seeking rest, the brain starts talking, flashing images of Jesse in our internal theatre and throwing around questions and random thoughts about his case. So Donna watches HGTV and I sit here pounding on the keyboard, trying to exorcise our demons. Donna who is more in touch with her inner self, knows this is coming and dreads November each year. I'm the guy who thinks it's better not to know what going on down there deep in my id(old sci fi movie reference *Forbidden Planet*), and so I am usually blind-sided by the rush of emotion and raw energy that comes flowing from within. The results are the same, we both will be a wreck before it is all over.

But we keep doing it, knowing that Jesse will simply become another 'missing' unless we do this. There will be press, and old friends of Jesse, and perhaps someone connected to his time in Chicago. Perhaps someone will suddenly recall an important fact; then we can go to Chicago, wake up the Keystone Kops and say here's your clue now get out there and do something. I do admit perhaps I am a bit hard on the forces of law and order, but 5 years of waiting can do that to you. I hope that my midnight ramblings bring some insight to you the reader. Perhaps if Jesse is still not here or we have no new clues by publishing time, one of you will be the messenger that brings us the news we so desperately crave. I also would ask that you not judge us too harshly for our 'parties'. There are no classes to prepare for this kind of thing and we do what we think will work. My wife and I both have experienced walking the paths that Jesse walked in Chicago, waiting and hoping to see him around the next corner. There is only so much the human heart can bear. And we or I will be back there again despite the feelings that are engendered.

November 11, 2011, Veterans day! Donna will go with me to Applebees for free lunch for veterans. It's all overshadowed by November 21st, 5th anniversary of Jesse's disappearance. My father, and my two brothers, all surviving veterans, and my son disappears on the streets of Chicago.

I would take his place in a minute. But it isn't my place to say what is to be or why. I think about the old friends I served with, wonder where they are, how many survived the Vietnam era. So much of life is loss, I guess we have to focus on what we have gained. Family, new friends; New babies coming into the world all around us. The babies I remember are having babies. My prayer is that the day will come when Jesse can join his family and friends and be a part of all this. No Jesse juniors for us, unless something changes.

November 20, 2011, Opiefest: Friday the 18th; At 3:pm we showed up at St. Regis church. I got the key for the Parish hall from the office. Donna, and myself were the only ones present in the beginning. We began by unloading signs, posters, tables, a laptop, all the things that go into such an event. We began by posting signs at the entrances. The Boy Scouts had their meeting the previous night and were kind enough to set up tables and chairs. We had to do some rearranging, but a lot of the work was done. Friends began to arrive soon and we had help; Placing more tables against the walls putting out displays; taping posters to the walls. Fortunately a friend had arranged for a laptop and projector, so we loaded a cd with Jesse's images for a slideshow. Soon there were 4 of us working, then six. Time moves quickly when you get involved in something this big. 5:30 and the band began to set up. Friends who were driving in from other parts of the state began to show. We set up a long set of tables and displayed raffle items. A 32 inch flat screen television, Gift cards, comfort packs featuring throws, dvd's, books signed by the authors.

Speaking of authors, our guest speaker, Michael Tabman showed up with his lovely wife. Michael is a former, police officer, FBI agent, and presently runs a private security firm. Michael graciously agreed to share his expertise on Law Enforcement, especially pertaining to the missing. We consider ourselves fortunate to have access to Michael's expertise and to count him as a personal friend. One of the items we raffled was a copy of Michael's second book, which he signed on site for the lucky winner.

This year we had 3 bands, *The Burnt Ends*, a group formed by members of our church, specializing in country music. *A Dead Giveaway,* Jesse's friends and a band deeply involved in the search for Jesse. They performed concerts, organized a tour, and walked the streets of Chicago with me, anything for the cause. This year they brought along another band called *The Paperclips*, two individuals with a huge sound. We were blessed in the music department with so many great sounds.

Meissens Catering Services appeared shortly before 6 and set out a meal fit for a king. The Meissens are friends from church, besides being a *class A* food service. We have used them as long as we have been gathering at the church for Opiefest. We have never been disappointed. Many additional items were donated by friends and family, making for a memorable event.

For Donna and I this is a mixed bag. We are inundated with reminders of Jesse's absence. It is a little bit like torturing ourselves. But we carry with us the memory of Jesse's zest for life, his naturally joyous outlook on all of life. We were determined to dedicate the evening to all that made Jesse the wonderful son that he was for all of 19 years.

Going through the house and gathering the various pieces that would put Jesse's signature on this event, I came across a print out of the email we received from one young lady. She was unsure why we were 'partying' when we should be out looking for Jesse. Certainly it was a hurtful thing to receive, but we had to think about how others perceive our actions. She asked a perfectly reasonable question. You have to be in our shoes to understand what it is like. We put on a circus, we wave Jesses name and face around for the world to see. We raise funds for travel, promotional, and other expenses; If we could only go to Chicago and take up the trail. If we could push police and demand action; drag them from behind their desks; prowl the dark streets of Chicago and 'roust' the suspicious characters of 'Chicago after dark'. But we are parents, family and we are limited in what we can do. We certainly have prowled the streets of Chicago; but he is not standing on a street corner; or hanging at the Navy pier; or wandering around the hotel. Opiefest is our strength. It is difficult to be thrust so strongly into the reality of our sorrow; so we make this event as positive as we can. We do not ask friends and family to come and beat themselves and wail and moan. We ask them to gather and bring their hope, and prayers and strength and all the positive energy they can. And we are renewed so we can continue to walk the streets, talk to the media, visit with local politicians and other families of the missing. Opiefest is a tribute to all that is good about our son.

One facet of this event is the presence of many of our new friends that Jesse has sent to us. Mothers, fathers, wives and husbands; children all having lost someone, all searching or dealing with the tragedy of a deceased loved one. Many are there with us, others gathered in Cyberspace, sending their best wishes when they were unable to attend in person. People dealing with death in the family, or illnesses, or obligations to other family members. I was taken back to when I stood in the lobby of the Sheraton Inn(where Jesse disappeared) in December of 2006,thinking of our Jesse, and our great sorrow, while surrounded by parents and happy children and all the decorations for Christmas. I again had to realize at Opiefest that the world does not stop turning. The sadness and unfortunate events of life are just a part of life. We have to rise above them and look beyond life's horizon. The young lady asks 'how can we party?' What else can we do? I have learned tears may sometimes be necessary, but they will not sustain us when we have to do the things life demands of us. Cry and you cry alone, smile and the world smiles with you. And these new friends serve as reminders that we are not alone, just how selfish we would be to center on only our sorrows.

Scattered around the parish hall are posters and 'table toppers', featuring pictures and facts related to missing persons from around the country. Some of the families and supporters of these missing were present with us that night. All taking comfort in the warmth and good feelings that are at the heart of Opiefest.

10:00 pm and the festivities are winding down. Volunteers help put away table and chairs and clean up. Hugs, kisses, tears, farewells; even talk of next year. In February we will travel to Wichita to celebrate February family birthdays(including Jesse's). But for this year, we will struggle thru Thanksgiving and Christmas with the support of friends and family. Opiefest is the 'Fiscal' year end for our Jesse activities, the time when we renew the hope that the next Opiefest will feature Jesse himself brought home to us whole and well.

PART THREE

THE FUTURE

CHAPTER 8

2011-

Epilogue

We have shared here the story of our son Jesse Ross, gone nearly 5 years ago in Chicago. Because we know so little of what has happened to Jesse, much of this book is dedicated to the story of those of us left behind. We would love to dedicate every chapter of this book to Jesse, but we can't since we are totally in the dark about Jesse's fate for all these years. There are many others as well who are no where to be found. This is more than a book; it is a challenge to all of us. To be advocates for those who cannot speak for themselves and to write the last chapter to this story. And all the unfinished stories that are still to be told.

"Before the people of the world, let it now be noted that here, in our decision, this is what we stand for: justice, truth, and the value of a single human being."—Spencer Tracy in *Judgment at Nuremberg, 1961*—Roxlom Films Inc.

If you would take nothing else from this book, take the quotation above. Those of us gathered to represent the missing, abused, abducted, murdered, and trafficked victims of the world, this is our statement; A worthy statement for the entire world. This book is not just about Jesse Ross. It is for all those whom we call victims. Just because all of us have not been affected, we still must believe that when one is hurt all are hurt. A crime against one person is a crime against all; It must be treated seriously, regardless of prejudices or apathetic leanings of some who are charged with the investigation of said crimes. As individuals we must be prepared to confront those who refuse to take seriously the plight of any person, whether we are directly involved or not.

Let these words burn into your heart

"We stand for . . . . the value of a single human being."

We would dearly love to give you a happy ending, as this is the last chapter of this book, the unfinished chapter. You will find a few empty pages here. We hope that someone out there will help write this final and most important chapter. My family looks for hope and peace and most of all the return of our beloved son. So to each of you, I say this is your opportunity to become a part of this story and to make the world right again. Thank you from the family and friends of Jesse 'Opie' Ross.

APPENDIX A

The People

Kelly Jolkowski

About the Founder and President of Project Jason, Kelly Jolkowski

Kelly Jolkowski, president and founder of Project Jason, is one of the foremost experts in the field of missing persons in the United States. She is one of the few non-law enforcement people trained at the criminal justice program at the premier college specializing in missing persons and has more than 100 hours of professional training on missing persons from the National Center for Missing and Exploited Children. The U.S. Department of Justice and Fox Valley Technical College.

She has been a speaker at events for National Center for Missing and Exploited Children, at the National Sex Offender Management Conference, Fox Valley's Uniting in the Search for the Missing, and the National Candlelight Vigil. She taught Project Jason's course on DNA and Missing Persons at the 2008 Cue Center Conference.

She frequently lectures about missing persons issues, law enforcement and missing persons, and the science of DNA and its benefits to finding missing persons.

She is also called to speak about laws affecting missing persons because of her leadership of Campaign for the Missing, which mandates how missing and unidentified persons are handled. It has been passed in eight states so far. She also speaks about her steerage of Jason's Law, which mandated the creation of the Nebraska State Missing Person's Clearinghouse.

In 2009, she was the recipient of the Keeper of the Flame award, given annually to law enforcement, business leaders, organizations, search personnel and/or volunteers who have risen above their daily duties in the field of missing persons and service to victims of homicide; persons who have shown great empathy and brought forth action for the cause. She has appeared on the Montel Williams Show, Fox National Dayside News, numerous national and international radio shows, and in USA Today.

In April of 2010, the U.S. Justice Department's Office for Victims of Crime (OVC) named Kelly Jolkowski as the Volunteer for Victims Honoree. The announcement came at the National Crime Victims' Service Awards Ceremony held in Washington, DC. The awards, given by US Attorney General Eric Holder, are part of the OVC's National Crime Victims Rights Week. Kelly was one of eight people honored by the U.S. Justice Department for their work assisting victims of crime.

She has developed several unique awareness programs to help locate the missing, including the 18 Wheel Angels, Awareness Angels Network, and Come Home. In addition, Kelly works daily with families of the missing nationwide through Project Jason and also with TEAM Hope, a branch of NCMEC.

The first retreat for families of the missing, Keys to Healing, was held in June of 2009. Kelly spent more than a year in development of the event, which is designed to give families of the missing the tools they need to take care of themselves emotionally and physically as they continue their searches. The retreat is now an annual event.

Kelly's work on behalf of families of the missing began in 2001 after her 19-year-old son, Jason, disappeared. At the time of his disappearance, Kelly and her husband Jim did not know where they could turn for assistance when Jason disappeared.

There were many things that, had they known back then, they would have done differently to more quickly and effectively search in the hours and days that followed. And they could have used a sympathetic ear.

After their experience, they determined that where there are other families in such need, they would be there for them. To do so, they founded the nonprofit Project Jason, Assistance for Families of the Missing.

While her ultimate goal is to be able to work for Project Jason full time in order to serve more families of the missing, Jolkowski serves Project Jason in the hours surrounding her full time job. The efforts to find her son continue on as a regular, although not normal, part of her life. (courtesy of Kelly Jolkowski)

Christina Fontana—Director/Producer

Christina has been working professionally in film and television for over 12 years. She began her career working in the assistant director dept. for many films including:+

The Station Agent (Miramax Films—Best Screenplay & Audience Award, Sundance 2003)

Coffee and Cigarettes (Director, Jim Jarmush)

Jersey Girl (Director, Kevin Smith)

The Motel (Best Screenplay, Sundance 2002)

(And a variety of television shows including)

Law and Order

America's Most Wanted.

While working as an assistant director on narrative projects seasoned Christina as a filmmaker, she decided to follow her passion of creatively prompting social awareness and change through documentary film. She has been working as an Editor on various documentary shows for networks such as FOX, The History Channel, Discovery, HBO, A&E, PBS and more. She also has credits on documentary films such as *A Walk to Beautiful* (named Best Feature Documentary of the Year-International Documentary Association 2007), *loudQUIETloud*: A Film about the Pixies (Official Selection, Tribeca Film Festival 2006), *James Blunt: Return to Kosovo* and the HBO film I *am an Animal: The Story of Ingrid Newkirk and PETA*. She is now turning her focus toward directing and continues to push herself to create social awareness through film.

View Full Filmography
http://www.imdb.com/name/nm1275601/resume

Project Jason: A Voice for the Missing(working title)
If you are over the age of 18 and you go missing in the United States, your hope of rescue is commonly placed in the hands of local law enforcement. In most states, if they don't know how or don't want to look for you, they won't. This film takes an intimate look inside the lives of families, across the country, who have been abandoned and sometimes even abused because of a failed system. Adults,

while they have the freedom to disappear if they choose, are also just as vulnerable to foul play as children are and should have the same right to be protected.

I was introduced to the issue of missing adults when my friend Alisa shared the story of how badly her missing brother's case was treated by police because he was 18 and considered an adult.

I will never forget the day she shared her story with me. We were on the roof of her east village apartment drinking beers and watching the sun go down. I had been friends with her for over a year and knew she had a brother who went missing but I never pressed her for details. Whenever she would share a piece of the story, I would listen. That day she told me the whole story. She told me how Jeffrey was a freshman in college when he asked his high school sweetheart to marry him.

She felt they were too young and didn't accept. He fell into a depression and left school. He started hanging around with his cousin who was a drug dealer and not the sort she wanted her little brother to be around.

In the late hours of Superbowl, Sunday 2001, Jeffrey disappeared. His cousin claimed Jeffrey left his house in his car alone. His car was later found within a few miles, but no Jeffrey. The details that followed are enough to fill an entire book (which Alisa is writing). It begins with the police telling her family that since Jeffrey had been 18 for over four months that he was an adult; and that he had the right to go missing, regardless of anonymous tips coming in that her cousin murdered her brother; and it ends with her family on a search six years later, after a tip came in from some loggers that they spotted skeletal remains on a mountain.

The police claimed that they had searched this area and found nothing; but they told the family they could have a look in the area if they wanted. Alisa was the first to find something. She said that she saw what looked like a piece of shirt and began digging with her bare hands around the area. She was tossing dirt and twigs when her mom stopped her and told her that one of the twigs she had in her hand wasn't a twig at all. It was a rib bone. She said, suddenly everything grew quiet; like the whole world fell away as she stared at the bone in her hand.

The bone was later identified as Jeffrey's.

I will never forget how I felt after she finished telling me the whole story. I knew at that moment I was about to dedicate the next few years of my life to the making of a documentary. A documentary that would show people what I had been blind to; about how adult missing person's cases are handled in our society.

After much research, I came across **Project Jason**; and about a year later I began filming. After 3 years and 130 hours of footage, I am close to completion of a project that I hope will make proud the many families I have met from all across the country. I am happy to say we have been able to create videos for non-profits needing to spread their word, organize and fund searches, and aid in getting media exposure for individual family's cases. No matter what journey the finished film takes, I will always be humbled by the journey I have taken in its creation. (courtesy of Christina Fontana)

Sara Huizenga

My name is Sara Huizenga, I am the founder **of Peace4 the Missing**.

I am also **NamUs Academy Victim Advocate for the State of Michigan**, co-owner and creative director of **Socialsprouts**, based out of Grand Haven, MI and was involved in Michigan's (May 7ᵗʰ, 2011 at Ford Fields, Detroit) first ever **Missing Person's Day**.

I have an education background of and currently professionally work in the communications field: media, publicity and social media, etc. I'm also the lucky to be Mom of two (most always ;-) sweet little girls, Anna age 9 and Maggie age 5.:).

I would just like to say the Ross family is a true testimony of what passion and persistence really can achieve.

(courtesy of Sara Huizenga)

Maureen Reintjes

Maureen Reintjes became a victims advocate for the families of the missing after enduring 4 years of a search for her own missing loved one (www.reintjes.us). Maureen is now the National Missing and Unidentified Persons System (NamUs) Victims

Advocate for Kansas. She is also an administrator for Peace4 the Missing. She has advocated for many families across the US and other countries by providing support, media liaison and awareness campaigns via social media. Maureen promotes the Help Find the Missing Act "Billy's Law" HR 1300 / SR 702 and has her own law that she maliciously missing. (courtesy of Maureen Reintjes)

Duane Bowers

Duane T. Bowers, LPC, CCHT is a Licensed Professional Counselor and Educator, and a Certified Clinical Hypnotherapist in private practice. He is the author of Guiding Your Family through Loss and Grief, and A Child is Missing: Providing Support for Families of Missing Children, and also hosted the live, call-in internet radio show LET'S TALK IT THROUGH.

As a therapist Duane's specialty is working with survivors of traumatic death and suicide, which includes assisting families who must identify loved ones at the DC Office of the Chief Medical Examiner, through the Wendt Center for Loss and Healing. He also provides support to families of abducted, missing, exploited and murdered children through the National Center for Missing and Exploited Children (NCMEC). In addition, Duane serves as a training consultant to NCMEC, and is deployed by them to provide crisis intervention at Amber Alert sites with Team Adam. He also serves as a consultant and trainer for Team HOPE, a telephone support line for parents of missing children, and has provided services to AMECO (Association of Missing and Exploited Children Organizations). Duane also works as a therapist with members of the military and their families through Military Onesource.

As an educator, Duane teaches seminars nationally, internationally and regionally on dying, death and grief, as well as trauma, Post Traumatic Stress Disorder (PTSD), and traumatic loss. He has served as an Adjunct Professor of Counseling at Trinity College in Washington DC, and has been an invited guest lecturer for national conferences, as well as for graduate and undergraduate classes of various colleges and universities. Duane is also a contract trainer for the Office for Victims of Crime.

Duane is responsible for the clinical supervision and training of staff and volunteers for a variety of organizations that deal with trauma and loss. He served as the Director of Training and Education at the Wendt Center for Loss and Healing in Washington DC, and was the Senior Director of Emergency and International Services for the National Capital Chapter of the American Red Cross. Duane spent three months during the summer of 1999 in Macedonia/ Kosovo/Albania supervising a family reunification program in camps with war refugees. In September 2001 Duane responded to the Pentagon immediately following the terrorist attack on September 11th, providing support to rescue and recovery workers. In April 2010 he served as the mental health team leader at the University of Miami field hospital following the earthquake in Port au Prince, Haiti.

Published works:

Bowers, D.T. (2009, Summer). Supporting your grieving pet. *American Academy of Bereavement News,* 2, 6.

Bowers, D.T. (2007). *A child is missing: Providing support for families of missing children.* Alexandria, VA: National Center for Missing and Exploited Children.

Greif, G. & Bowers, D. (2007). Unresolved loss: Issues in working with adults whose siblings were kidnapped years ago. *The American Journal of Family Therapy,* vol. 35, issue 3, pp. 203-219.

Bowers, D.T. (2005). *Guiding your family through loss and grief.* Tucson, AZ: Fenestra Books.

Bowers, D.T. (2005) *Information for families grieving after the loss of a child, and the professionals who support them.* Retrieved February 3, 2005. http://www.missingkids.com/en_US/publications/NC10.pdf

Bowers, D. T. (2002). *Communicating with someone who is grieving.* American

Association of Retired Persons (AARP), web-site, www.aarp.org/griefandloss/articles/103_a.hml, 1-4.

(courtesy of Duane Bowers)

A Dead Give Away

A Dead Giveaway started out like most high school rock bands; a group of friends who simply wanted to play music like those they admired. In the beginning there were many obstacles, learning to play the instruments being a major one. It was the winter of 2001/2002 when the first elements of band started to gather, at the time the boys were only freshman in High School; discovering a new world of creativity and life. The original line up of the band consisted of 4 members. Two of whom (Brandon Woodall and Bryce Veazey) are still members today. In those early days the main priority of the band was covering songs that had already achieved popularity with other bands. This technique allowed the young musicians to explore the dynamics of songwriting without having to actually write the songs; a task that is overwhelmingly daunting, even to those who make carriers out of playing music.

As time proceeded, the band's line-up changed. Eventually resting on the 5-member line up that it is today. In it's current state, A Dead Giveaway consists of: Jesse Collins (lead vocals), Cory Tittle (Bass), Brandon Woodall (Drums/Percussion), Jon Gibbens (Guitar/Keys) and Bryce

Veazey (Guitar/Backing Vocals). A Dead Giveaway has maintained it's current line up for the past 8 years.

Once a firm line up for the band solidified, the group began its true mission; writing impassioned meaningful music that spoke directly to the listener. The first songs that were written by A Dead Giveaway bridged a gap for the band. This burst of personal creation eventually eliminated the need to learn cover songs, bringing the band into an identity and persona all its own. As the band grew through many avenues in it's early days; one in particular being the building of relationships with those outside of the 5 members who populated the band. Anyone who has been around the music industry knows that it's not "what you know, but who you know". This cliché was proven all too true for A Dead Giveaway.

In his high school years, drummer Brandon Woodall held a job working for a local movie theater. It was at this job that Woodall met a person that would alter and influence the direction of A Dead Giveaway in years to come. Jesse "Opie" Ross was also an employee at the movie theater and after meeting Woodall, Opie became increasingly interested in A Dead Giveaway. In the years that followed, Opie grew close to the band, booking shows for them, traveling with the band to out of town gigs and altogether supporting the group as they grew. By the time that A Dead Giveaway was out of High School, Opie had been a stand in manager for close to 3 years; practically a sixth member in the group.

When the news of Opie's disappearance reached A Dead Giveaway, the reality took some time to sink in. Naturally there were elements of disbelief and shock, which eventually gave way to grief and sorrow. However, A Dead Giveaway had experience with the loss of a close friend. In the fall of 2004 a dear friend, Chris Gammon, was killed in a car accident. The band was deeply affected and moved into action by Gammon's death; organizing a benefit concert and dedicating an entire album to Gammon.

This experience had instilled a sense of duty and responsibility in the band; a dedication to those who have been hurt or are suffering. In the months that followed Opie's disappearance, the band began to develop a way in which they could help.

Saturday May 26th, 2007 was the beginning of Opiefest, a series of benefit concerts that aim to shed light on Opie's case, as well as other missing persons. Opiefest continued to grow over the years, all the while keeping Opie's story in the spotlight. Each event makes distinct efforts to receive publicity from local and national news organizations, highlighting the importance of keeping a vigilant and aggressive focus on the issue.

In the summer of 2010, A Dead Giveaway took Opiefest on the road, staging a 10-day Midwest tour called "Opie's Tour". The tour brought media attention to Opie's story in nearly every area it visited. Through a unrelenting passion, the band had taken Opie's story further than it had ever been before. The tour culminated in Chicago, the location of Opie's disappearance. A Dead Giveaway returned to Kansas City feeling that they had fulfilled some degree of their desires with the tour, yet still the sting of missing Opie hung heavy over the group. Local Opiefests continued the following winter, again reminding the community of Opies Story. In years to come, Opiefest will remain a staple in A Dead Giveaway's identity, even as the band moves forward into adulthood, their dedication to Opie and his family, will remain true. (courtesy of A Dead Giveaway)

APPENDIX B

Internet

Here are some items of interest from the internet.

This is an example of the international exposure Jesse obtained. I have no clue what it says, I think it is Greek?

28619. Jesse Ross χαμένος
and updated: 9/1/07 1013 ET

Jesse Ross χαμένος μέσα κομμός, μόλις κάνω ένα web ψάχνω επάνω Jesse Ross χαμένος αποκτώ λεπτομέρεια. όπως μας προσευχή είναι με εκείνοι ποιός απολεσθείς so much μέσα όχι.

———◦◦◦◦◦◦———

On Myspace April 30,2007 Freelance writer Brandon Johnson contacted us wanting to do an article on Jesse.

———◦◦◦◦◦◦———

https://www.oprah.com/plugger/templates/. BeOnTheShow.jhtml?action+respond&plugid+B210004 This is the link we were given for the Oprah show. Donna and I and many of our friends emailed Oprah in the hope of getting some exposure for Jesse. We never got so much as a 'No' 'Go to Hell' or 'glad to help' I find her so-called generous reputation to be so much hypocrisy.

———◦◦◦◦◦◦———

http://www.957thevibe.com/vibe.shtml This is no longer a valid URL, but at one time you could go here listen to music live, and see Jesse on the webcam. Oh that we could do that and see our boy again. This is the latest link to Shorty and the boys web-based radio program http://www. shortyandtheboyzradio.com

⚬⚬⚬⚬⚬⚬⚬⚬⚬

http://findjesseross.com
This is currently the webpage for Jesse. It contains pictures, text information, and a feature to purchase hats, t-shirts, buttons, etc.

⚬⚬⚬⚬⚬⚬⚬⚬⚬

http://footprintsattheriversedge.blogspot.com
This site contains information about two former police detectives who linked together several homicides of young college men. They offered the theory of a serial killer or killers, who were leaving a 'happy face' symbol near the place where they tossed the bodies of young men into various bodies of water. Our PI looked for graffiti in Chicago, but we learned that Chicago employed a company to remove graffiti from public structures. Jesse has been included in this group but we have never seen any evidence that he might be victim of such a plot.

⚬⚬⚬⚬⚬⚬⚬⚬⚬

http://www.projectjason.org The website for Project Jason.

⚬⚬⚬⚬⚬⚬⚬⚬⚬

www.missingkids.com Website for National Center For Missing and Exploited Children.

Sample pages from 'missing Jesse Ross' search

Help Us Find Jesse Ross

Any information regarding the disappearance of Jesse Ross . . . Missing and Exploited Children Site regarding Jesse; Additional Case Information findjesseross.com—Cached

AMW | Missing Persons | Jesse Ross | Brief

Missing Persons | Jesse Ross—Brief—Successful Student Vanishes Jesse Ross was on his way to success The student managed school work a job in radio and his social . . . www.amw.com/missing_persons/brief.cfm?id=42565—Cached

Missing Jesse Ross | Facebook

Missing Jesse Ross—Last seen 11/21/2006 in downtown Chicago . . . please call with info 312-744-8266 $10,000 Reward | Facebook www.facebook.com/jesseopieross—Cached

Missing

JESSE ROSS : DOB: Feb 18, 1987 Missing: Nov 21, 2006 Age Now: 24 Sex: Male Race: White Hair: Red Eyes: Blue Height: 5'10" (178 cm) Weight: 140 lbs (64 kg) www.missingkids.com/missingkids/servlet/PubCaseSearchSe . . .—Cached

Missing Jesse Ross—Info | Facebook

Missing Jesse Ross—Last seen 11/21/2006 in downtown Chicago . . . please call with info 312-744-8266 $10,000 Reward | Facebook www.facebook.com/jesseopieross?sk=info—Cached

National Center for Missing & Exploited Children

JESSE ROSS: Age Progression Case Type: Missing : DOB: Feb 18, 1987: Sex: Male: Missing Date: Nov

ity

21, 2006: Race: White: Age Now: 24: Height: 5'10"
(178 cm) www.missingkids.com/missingkids/servlet/
PubCaseSearchSe . . .—Cached

AMW | Missing Persons | Jesse Ross | Brief
Missing Persons | Jesse Ross—Brief—Successful
Student Vanishes Jess . . . www.amw.com/missing_persons/
brief.cfm?id=42565
Missing Jesse Ross | Facebook
Missing Jesse Ross—Last seen 11/21/2006 in downtown
Chicago . . . pleas . . . www.facebook.com/jesseopieross
Missing
JESSE ROSS : DOB: Feb 18, 1987 Missing: Nov
21, 2006 Age Now: 24 Sex: . . . www.missingkids.com/
missingkids/servlet/PubCaseSearchServlet?act=viewPoster
&caseNum=1067881&orgPrefix=NCMA&searchLang=
en_US
More Sponsors:
missing Jesse Ross,
missing
Search results
Crime Scene KC—Kansas City's Best Source for News,
Weather . . .
Thank You James Hart for the Article about My Sweet
Friends Missing Son Jesse "Opie" Ross. He is Missed &
Loved By Many!! blogs.kansascity.com/crime_scene/2010/
11/opiefest-to . . .—Cached
Monday4 the Missing: Jesse Warren Ross "Opie"
Jesse Ross looks like the "All American" college kid, a
good kid, who with red hair, freckles and an infectious smile
earned him the nickname, "Opie". monday4themissing.
blogspot.com/2008/12/jesse-warren-ross . . .—Cached

Chris's Crime Forum • View topic—Jesse Ross: missing
b a black cloud settled in over us and the nightmare began'
b help us find jesse warren ross missing since november last
seen sheraton hotel and towers in . . .

Jesse Ross-Missing From Chicago, IL by The Missing
Project . . .
Read Jesse Ross—Missing From Chicago, IL by The
Missing Project on Myspace. Social entertainment powered
by the passions of fans. www.myspace.com/missingproject/
blog/259478347—Cached

Bands play for missing UMKC student Jesse Ross
Missing > Missing Adults . . . http://www.kctv5.com/
news/18749306/detail.html Missing Student's Parents
Hold Onto . . . http://findjesseross.com/ . . . http://www.
suntimes . . . helpfindthemissing.org/forum/showthread.
php?p=790118—Cached

Illinois Missing Persons Day
Propelled by the horrific experience of a missing son
of their own, Jesse 'Opie' Ross, the efforts from Don and
Donna Ross have now transpired into an official Missing
and . . . illinoismissingpersonsday.blogspot.com—Cached

Sponsored Results
Missing Man: Jesse Ross—IL—11/21/2006
Age progressed to 22 years Police Seek Help To Find
Missing Missouri St . . . projectjason.org/forums/index.
php?topic=729.0

GINA For Missing Persons—Jesse Warren Ross
MISSING PERSON PROFILE Endangered Missing
Adult: Name: JESSE WARREN RO . . . www.411gina.org/
jessewarrenross.htm

Jesse Ross Vanished Without a Trace in 2006 | True
Crime Diva

This entry was posted in Missing Adults and tagged Chicago, Jesse Ross, . . . truecrimediva.com/?p=648

Twenty year old Jesse Ross, University of Missouri at KS . . .

21 year old Jesse Ross has been missing in Chicago, IL since early Tues . . . missingexploited.com/2006/11/27/ twenty-year-old-jesse-ross-university-of-missouri-at-ks-student-missing-in-chicago-il/

APPENDIX C

POEMS

(Not mine)

"Jesse Ross's Unfinished Song" by Bob Rich,

*m*usic gives rhythm to Jesse each day
through radio shows he liked to DJ
And concerts he planned that starred a friend's band
While touring with them, he'd lend them a hand.

Sports provide Jesse with good energy
Track and Cross County, he'd run patiently
Snack stands he worked were at ball fields nearby
He proved that, in sales, his strong talents fly.

His outgoing ways made college years fun
Forging good friendships, he's second to none
He'd help to put on the campus events
Media studies for Jesse made sense.

Family time, he quite often would seek
Movies, he'd go to with brother each week
He and his dad dined at Chili's in style
He and his mom watched cartoons for a smile.

For chances to give, he often would search
Like when he arranged fundraisers for church

(song)

> *Some broken hearts never mend*
Some memories never end.
Some tears will never dry my love for you will never die.
—*Don Williams*

> *-I loved you the minute I heard you were coming-I loved you the minute you were born, then I saw your face and I fell in love some more. You were only a minute old, but I knew I would die for you-to this day I still would. When you choose to have a child you make a conscious decision to allow your heart to walk around n outside your body.—from the Internet, no idea who said it.*

AT FIRST WHEN YOU WERE GONE
At first when you were gone I turned my face
From life and sat upon a lonely place
And then above my sorrow and my strife
I found the Resurrection and the Life.
Robert Norwood (excerpt).

CONSOLATION
He is not dead, this friend; not dead. but, in the path we mortals tread,

Gone some few trifling steps ahead,
And nearer to the end;
So that you, too, once past the bend,
Shall meet again, as face to face, this friend
You fancy dead.
Robert Louis Stevenson

———————

(Mine)

The Waiting Room

Not the doctor or dentist kind,
Not that kind of room
A room that waits.

A living room, but not that kind
A room that lives, contains the life force
Of the one for whom it waits.

Does it callout in the night(we do).
A beacon shining into the night
Calling "Come home".

The waiting room.
Sadly not the only one.

Dreams—*Donald Ross*

Dreams oh so warm and sweet
Memories of past friends flow
With open hearts and hugs we meet
The mellow sunlight has a glow

Then reality's arrives bright and slick
To poke me in the eyes,
With a sharpened stick.

But I will rise, and meet the day
Chase away the fright
Once more make my way
To dream another night.

The Whistle

Here you see a whistle
It's sound is loud and shrill
You can hear it in the valley
You can hear it on the hill

Came from some Cracker Jacks
Many year ago
Oh the trouble it would make
No one could really know.

A boy named Jesse
Played it in the day
Played it late at night
Play, play, play

I Finally had to take it
I have it even now
And the boy is gone
We know not where or how
I find myself tempted to stand

Donald Ross

In the yard alone
To blow that awful whistle
Saying "Jesse please come home".

In Springfield

Walking the halls
In the Antique malls
voices floating on the wind
from the east,
just around the bend
I pay them no mind
Just echoes in time
Voices from the mist,
of People and places
that no longer exist
Just in our memory,
and places yet to be

————～～●◦●◆◎◆●◦●～～————

<u>Where's Opie</u>

By <u>Donald Andrew Ross</u> · Monday, November 29, 2010
Grandma Madeline talked to the news,
before she died
With questions about Jesse,
on the air she cried . . . .
Where's Opie?

Loan collector's wrote us and
called on the phone
With questions about Jesse,
was he home . . . .
Where's Opie?

The one caller from his school,
she seemed a little dim.
We said he was missing, she said
"okay, but could you ask him . . . ."

Jesse, Jesse Where are you?

Jesse, Jesse where you gone?
The morning bird's lost it's song
The morning sky's no longer blue
Jesse, Jesse where are you?

Chicago ain't my kind of town
Til they say that you been found.
I want to know this very day,
Who it is took you away.

Where you gone? To outer space?
Or off to war to be an ace:
Jesse, Come on home to us
Give a call, we'll grab the bus.

Life's not the same it isn't whole
There's such a pain within our soul
So find your way, come back again
Find a way to heal our pain.

Donald Ross

Jesse, Jesse where you gone?
The morning bird's lost it's song
The morning sky's no longer blue
Jesse, Jesse where are you?

―――❦―――

Baby Boy

Held you in my arms
When you were born
Tho you waited til
Early morn

Presented you to God
Asked his blessing
He gave you his nod.

Took you first day to school
They taught you to read and write
And the golden rule.

Soccer and track, scouting too
Such a busy boy
That was you.

―――❦―――

Left too soon

My dad you left us too soon
Only 73 years young
Your day ended at noon
Your song was not sung.

Wish you were here
We lost our Jesse
you loved him so dear.
You gave him your blessing.

Now up in heaven
you look down on us all
Look for our Jesse
Please hear our call.

If he is in heaven
Show him around
If he is not
Please let him be found

As a boy I looked to you
for answers a many
just what I should do
your wisdom was uncanny

So hear our plea father
and put in a word
with the Holy father
lest he has not heard.

Donald Ross

THE RIDE

Board the Carousel
Enjoy the ride.
Pick a horse
And sit astride

But know this
It seems a curse
It stops for no one
Nor does it reverse

You buy a ticket
Your course is set
No room for if,
Nor for regret.

And when the ride
Has come to an end.
the mind is slow
The back did bend

Again know this,
It is only a ride,
There is more to come
Take all in stride.

There is a thing
Called hope
It rides with us
Helps us cope.

Until the day
When all is right,
Our final ride,
To eternal light.

D. A. Ross

———————

Ride the Wild Wind—Donald Ross

Ask any old cowboy
He'll tell you its so

You ain't ridin'
Til you are decidin'

Where and when to go

There's only one boss
The man or the hoss

So it is with life,
Living each day,
We have to find,
Each our own way.

Dedicated to my sons Andy and Jesse Ross

To the Mountains—Donald Ross

*I would go to the mountains
In search of sweet rest,
Blue skies and green meadows
Mother Nature at best.
Cool breezes, swift waters,
Snow on the peaks,
Serene, quiet moments where
God only speaks.*

*I would go to the mountains
To gain a respite,
Wile others continue to bicker and fight.
To spend all my days
'til death comes to call
And lifts me to heaven,
The sweetest mountain of all.*   Pre Jesse

———ww•o•e•o•o•o•o•ww———

Almost fishing—Donald Ross

*Quiet afternoon, some,
Time to write.
Jesse sleeps at last*

*Andy's at preschool Donna's
On the phone, the
Uproar is past.*

*Snow and ice cover the
Ground, Winter is here
Tho late*

Christmas is gone, I'm
Ready for spring The fish and I
Have a date.
Written when Jesse was a baby.

———www•ᴏ੨ᵗᴏᴏᵗᴈᴏ•www———

Serenade at seven am Donald Ross

Daii! Daii! (Dad)
Kookoo! Kookoo . . . . (cookie)
Mom! Mom! . . . . (you got that one)
AnNee! AnNee! . . . . (Andy andy)
Derder! Derder! . . . . (cookie, cookie)—A Jesse original, put
my name to it.

Life goes Round—Donald Ross

Some carry life
On their backs,
Like a bag full
Of bricks.

I prefer to roll It along
Like Children of yore
With their hoops
And sticks.

———www•ᴏ੨ᵗᴏᴏᵗᴈᴏ•www———

In the dark of early morn—Donald Ross

In the dark of early morn
Another working day is born.

Dreary drear and plainly plain
Scowling clouds and falling rain.

Still I find a cause for joy,
I kiss my wife and two sleeping boys.—started out one boy,
but Jesse insisted I change it. Glad I did.

⚬⚬⚬

Of children—Donald Ross

Who could harm a child?
What monster or beast?

Death of innocence,
Naivety deceased.

Could hell burn so hot?
To equal the deed?

Or heaven bring healing,
Fulfilling the need?

Let my weapon be prayer,
For God's will to be.

Lest Anger consume,
The best part of me.—Written long before Jesse disappeared.
A premonition?

———❧———

The Weewack brothers—Donald Ross

The Weewack brothers
Sleeping angels
So it seems

Are they just
As Ornery,
In their dreams?—Their mama called them that, Weewack

———❧———

Memory—Donald Ross

Memory is both,
A time and a place

A touch, a scent,
A smiling face.

A home, a loved one
A moment well spent.

A thing to be treasured
A gift to be lent.—old poem of mine.

———❧———

Quiet—Donald Ross

The silence of the house
At close of day,

Little ones sleep.
The dogs tucked away.

Mama and Daddy both
Breathe a sigh.

Tho both are aware,
That 'morning' is nigh.

On and On—Donald Ross

I know you hurt my friends
Had I your loss, I would hurt too.

Sons, and daughters, mothers and fathers
Victims of anger, Mars takes his due.

You bury your grief in hate
You bring grief to others,
Check and mate.

When does it stop?
When does it end?

When we forgive our brothers,
And call each other friend.—Written before I had my own
grief to bear.

Hand-me-down—Donald Ross

Like a modern day Frankenstein,
These parts I have they are not mine.

My father's eyes, my mother's nose,
Grandma's hair, my father's toes.

Contributions from Auntie this and uncle that,
My temper from the family cat.

Is there no part to call my own,
Borrowed skin and passed down bone.

As sad as this may sound,
I'm truly just a hand-me-down. And I handed down to my sons.

Andy and Opie—Donald Ross

Andy—hair like Kansas wheat.
Tall slender, a spattering of freckles.

Sensitive and possessed.

Donald Ross

———ᘛ·ᘚ———

Jesse-Hair the color of the setting sun,

A field of freckles,

A never ending stream of chatter.

Raw emotions flying this way and that.

Opie Taylor.—To my boys

———ᘛ·ᘚ———

Passages—Donald Ross

Have you ever had
The feeling,
Of something missed?

Passing by, in the corner
Of your eye?

*When this occurs, next **time***
Look for the answer,
In this rhyme.

———ᘛ·ᘚ———

Jesse—Donald Ross

We felt the loss. We felt the pain

I put myself into a box.
I did not like it in the box

So, I put my pain into
The box, instead.

I opened the box, and let
My pain go.
A little at a time. After Chicago.

─ww•ↄ੪ᴕⓄↂᴕↄ•ww─

First Christmas without—Donald Ross

Donna decorates the tree.

Outside the quiet serenity
Of a snow covered day.

Perhaps it could be a little
Less serene . . . .
Perhaps,
The sound of heavy bass
Thumping up from the basement.

The sound of a pair of size '11's
Clomping up the stairs.—silence can be a terrible thing.

─ww•ↄ੪ᴕⓄↂᴕↄ•ww─

Donald Ross

Early Years—Donald Ross

In early years, we found,
You woke us with your noise
The busy sound,
Of rowdy boys.

We took for granted that
You were here
At home we sat,
We knew no fear.

Now no noise you make
For you're not around
And we now awake;
To the lack of sound.

You are missed.

Together

We've come many miles
You and I love
Sighs or smiles,
Sun or clouds above

We've lost some, many storms
We've had to weather
Had some to mourn
But we are still together.

Love will keep us together

About the Author

Donald Ross was born June 27th, 1948 in Mansfield Missouri and raised in Wichita, KS. He attended Peabody High School in Peabody Kansas; He has about 35 hours of Computer-related college credits; He served in the US Army in the '60's and '70's, was a dishwasher, police officer, security guard, construction worker, accounting clerk, and finally became a Data Processing Associate for AT&T. In 1981 he met his wife to be Donna and they were married in 1982. In 1984, son Andy Ross was born; in 1987, son Jesse Ross was born. On November 21st, 2006, at age 19, Jesse disappeared in Chicago Illinois while attending a school sponsored Model UN conference. The Ross' are retired and living in Belton Missouri. This is Mr. Ross' first book, based on his experiences as the father of a missing person.